I0187273

Mixed Race Student Politics

A Rising "Third Wave" Movement at UCLA

Edited by Robert Chao Romero, James Ong,
Chelsea Guillermo-Wann, & Jenifer Logia

Copyright © 2019 Robert Chao Romero, James Ong, Chelsea Guillermo-Wann, Jenifer Logia and UCLA Asian American Studies Center.

3230 Campbell Hall
405 Hilgard Ave., Box 951546
Los Angeles, CA 90095-1546
(310) 825-2974

All rights reserved. No part of this book may be reproduced, stored, or transmitted by any means—whether auditory, graphic, mechanical, or electronic—without written permission of the author, except in the case of brief excerpts used in critical articles and reviews. Unauthorized reproduction of any part of this work is illegal and is punishable by law.

This book is a work of non-fiction. Unless otherwise noted, the author and the publisher make no explicit guarantees as to the accuracy of the information contained in this book and in some cases, names of people and places have been altered to protect their privacy.

ISBN: 978-0-9340-5252-8 (sc)

Library of Congress Control Number: 2018961138

Because of the dynamic nature of the Internet, any web addresses or links contained in this book may have changed since publication and may no longer be valid. The views expressed in this work are solely those of the author and do not necessarily reflect the views of the publisher, and the publisher hereby disclaims any responsibility for them.

All photos provided courtesy of interviewees.

Chao Romero, Robert, James Ong, Chelsea Guillermo-Wann, and Jenifer Logia, eds. *Mixed Race Student Politics: A Rising "Third Wave" Movement at UCLA*. Los Angeles: UCLA Asian American Studies Center, 2019.

Lulu Publishing Services rev. date: 10/02/2019

Contents

To mixed race students at UCLA, past and present—our time has come

Acknowledgments

This book is deeply personal and academically far-reaching, and would not have been possible without the support of many good people. Special thanks is owed to David K. Yoo, vice provost of the Institute of American Cultures (IAC), who has supported this project from its inception. The UCLA Chicano Studies Research Center (CSRC) and Asian American Studies Center (AASC) also supplied important financial support at a critical time in the form of an IAC research grant. Thank you CSRC director Chon Noriega for whole-heartedly embracing this non-traditional "Asian-Latino" mixed race academic project. Many rounds of thanks are also owed to the UCLA AASC. First, to the AASC Press. We are honored to publish this volume as part of the AASC Press and its important academic legacy. Thank you Karen Umemoto, Keith Camacho, Melany De La Cruz-Viesca, Mary Uyematsu Kao, and Barbra Ramos for your important leadership in the Center, Press, and field of Asian American Studies. Much thanks is further owed to the anonymous reviewers whose suggestions helped make this a much stronger project, as well as to Esperanza Terrell for her excellent work in copyediting.

The editors also wish to extend our gratitude to former vice chancellor of Student Affairs, Janina Montero, and assistant vice chancellor of Student Development, Suzanne Seplow. You helped us cast a vision for the importance of this book within the field of Student Affairs, and your generosity helped first get this project off the ground.

In its humble way, this book contributes to the growing field of mixed race studies. The editors are deeply appreciative of mixed race scholars such as Lane Hirabayashi, G. Reginald Daniels, Paul Spickard, Rudy Guevarra, Jr., Caroline Streeter, and Evelyn Hu-De Hart who have paved the way for us and many others over the past three decades. Your intellectual imprint may be found on every page of this book.

Finally, we wish to express our profound gratitude to all the contributors of this volume, as well as the Mixed Student Union at UCLA. This is your story. This is your movement. We are so privileged to be a part.

Robert Chao Romero
James Ong
Chelsea Guillermo-Wann
Jenifer Logia

A Rising "Third Wave" Movement of Mixed Race Student Politics at UCLA

Introduction

Robert Chao Romero

I'm a "Chino-Chicano." I was born in East Los Angeles and raised in Hacienda Heights, California. My father is an immigrant from Chihuahua, Mexico, and my mother an immigrant from Hubei, in Central China. I've been mixed race at UCLA for more than two decades.

When I first entered UCLA as a freshman in 1990, I explicitly denied my mixed race heritage because of stigma I experienced as a child. As an elementary school student in the recently desegregated public schools of Los Angeles, I was once told by a white classmate, "Me Chinese, me play joke, me do pee pee in your Coke." That experience, among others, caused me to believe that being Chinese was a bad thing and caused me to claim a monoracial Mexican American identity until my mid-twenties. I first came to "claim" my Chinese ancestry as a third year law student at U.C. Berkeley after attending a Chinese immigrant church and forming close friendships with other Chinese Americans.

On an academic level, I first began exploring my Chinese and Mexican historical roots as a history graduate student at UCLA. I learned that Chinese, and other Asian descent groups, had lived in Latin America since the 1600s because of the Manila Galleon trade and U.S. exclusionary laws such as the Chinese Exclusion Act of 1882 and the Asiatic Barred

Zone Act of 1917. I learned that Chinese immigrants formed the second largest foreign ethnic community in all of Mexico during the first half of the twentieth century, and unfortunately, that they were also the targets of brutal anti-Chinese campaigns, which led to their expulsion from the state of Sonora in 1930. I also discovered that the Chinese were the first "undocumented immigrants" from Mexico. These findings became the basis of my dissertation and eventual book on the Chinese of Mexico.[1] As a UCLA professor of Chicana/o studies and Asian American studies, I have argued for the development of "Asian-Latino studies."

On a personal and academic level, my mixed race explorations led me to the study of theology. As a scholar of religious studies, I have explored the Christian scriptures to find answers to my many questions about race, ethnicity, and identity. After many years of reflection, I found a simple yet healing answer rooted in the theological concept of the "imago Dei," or the image of God. I reflect the image of God in my own unique way, and I am God's child. The image of God in me encompasses all of who I am—my Chinese, Mexican, and American heritages (Revelation 21: 26); my gender (Genesis 1:27); as well as my distinct personality, gifts, talents, and abilities (Psalm 139). All of these things together make me who I am. I can't divide myself into disparate parts—racial, cultural, or otherwise. I can't disaggregate myself. I wasn't intended to. All of these qualities make me a unique reflection of the image of God, and God's unique child. This meta-religious identity successfully integrates all of my cultural components. In this simple theological understanding, I am whole.[2]

My academic and personal reflections upon mixed race identity came crashing together for the first time in an undergraduate seminar I taught in 2014, titled, "Being Mixed Race at UCLA." The seminar explored a simple question: "What is it like being a mixed race student at UCLA?" This course offered me the chance to hear, first-hand, about the racial climate issues impacting multiethnic students at UCLA. I also learned about the important campus organizing efforts of the UCLA Mixed Student Union. With little exception, I came to understand that the racial climate concerns of the growing mixed race student population at UCLA had been largely overlooked. This conspicuous void led James Ong (graduate student of Asian American Studies and teaching assistant for the course), Jenifer Logia (student in the class and foundational leader of the Mixed Student

Union), and I, to first conceive of the idea for this book. Our simple vision was to publish an essay collection, which would give academic and political voice to multiracial students at UCLA. As we reflected upon whom else we might bring on to the project to provide scholarly guidance, we immediately thought of Chelsea Guillermo-Wann, who had recently completed a path-breaking dissertation on mixed race campus climate at UCLA.[3] The four of us soon formed an editorial team, and this volume of mixed race student stories is the result.

Building upon my own mixed-race counterstory, the fourteen student essays, which follow, offer a window into the diverse experience of being mixed race at UCLA.[4] Together, the essays evince a "third wave" of a new mixed race movement, as well as a rising tide of mixed race politics.[5] In response to a sense of "racial homelessness" fueled by the limited universe of monoracial institutional structures which define the campus, the authors declare with a unified voice that the rigid monoethnic racial lines of white, Black, Asian, and Latina/o no longer capture the social reality of UCLA or the United States.

At a size of more than nine million, the multiracial population of the United States is large and growing at an exponential rate. Between 2000 and 2010, the mixed race population grew by 32 percent.[6] This stands in contrast to the parallel growth of only 9 percent within the monoracial population. The Census Bureau projects that the multiracial population will triple by 2060, and it is estimated that as much as 20 percent of the entire U.S. population will be mixed race by 2050.[7] In fact, in the near future, the growth of the mixed race population will outpace that of Asians, Latinos, whites, Blacks, and Native Americans.[8] The United States is in the early stages of a profound racial and ethnic "mestizaje," in which cultural groups from every continent on the globe are freely mixing in a historically unprecedented way.

In 2010, the largest multiracial populations were found in the states of California (1,815,384), New York (585,849), and Texas (679,001). Regionally, the Western and Southern United States were home to 3.4 million, and 2.8 million individuals of mixed race ancestry, respectively. Sixteen states recorded multiracial populations of 200,000 or more, and multiple race respondents were found to reside in every county in the nation.[9] Los Angeles was home to the second largest population of mixed race individuals after New York City, and the larger metro Los Angeles area comprising Los Angeles-Long Beach-Riverside celebrated a mixed race population of more than 800,000.[10]

The rapid growth of the multiracial community is a direct reflection of increasing rates of cross-racial intermarriage. In 2010, 15 percent of all new marriages in the United States were between spouses of different races or ethnicities, and 9 percent of whites and 17 percent of Blacks married out. Among Latinos and Asians, outmarriage rates are even more staggering--more than 40 percent of recent Latino and Asian marriages are multiracial.[11] In 2010, these percentages translated into 1.8 million marriages between those of the white and Black race, 1.7 million marriages between white and some other race, 1.6 million white and Asian marriages, and 1.4 million marriages between those of the white and American Indian race.[12]

Against this backdrop of exponential multiracial growth on a national, state, and local level, UCLA operates almost exclusively as a monoracial space. The monoracial paradigm of race, which prevails on the UCLA campus, reflects the traditional identity politics of the civil rights era of the 1960s and 70s, and is in desperate need of update. As predicted by Homi Bhaba more than two decades ago, such monolithic identities do not accurately capture the scope of the cultural and political realities of racial hybrid subjects in the twenty-first century.[13]

The four ethnic studies centers at UCLA came of origin as a critical and necessary corrective to the outright racism, which characterized the university of the 1960s. As the academic outgrowth of the broader civil rights movement, Chicano, Asian American, Black, and American Indian students fought for the creation of distinct academic units and curricula devoted to the study of communities of color. They also demanded the hiring of faculty of color and the development of proactive policies aimed at increasing the representation of minority students on the college campus. These institutional changes were also accompanied by the formation of critical student retention services and initiatives such as the Academic Advancement Program.

By and large, these student groups and various administrative structures were organized along the lines of the dominant monoracial cultural and political identities of the time—Chicano, Asian American, Black, and American Indian. These social identities were both innovative and powerful, and responded directly to the racism and assimilationist politics of the era. For example, in reaction to the Latino assimilationist politics of the time, which favored whiteness and a "Spanish" cultural identity, university students of Mexican descent pushed back with the articulation of a new "Chicano" identity. As "Chicanos," they asserted cultural pride in both their indigenous and Spanish heritages and dedicated themselves to the socio-economic and political empowerment of the Mexican American community. In a similar fashion, the social identity of "Asian American" emerged in the 1960s, out of UCLA, as a pan-Asian American political and cultural identity.

The four ethnic studies centers at UCLA, as well as their respective departments and inter-departmental programs, still play a vital role. They promote and support critical research pertaining to the Chicana/o, Latina/o, Asian American, African American, and Native American communities; they produce top-notch undergraduate and graduate students who go on to important careers in academia, community organizing, law, public policy, medicine, and education.

At the same time, however, the four ethnic studies centers, standing alone, do not effectively encompass the broad ranging backgrounds and academic interests of the rising mixed race student community.[14] Existing administrative structures throughout the UCLA campus, moreover, are also based upon a limited monoracial paradigm. On an institutional level, mixed race students at UCLA find themselves alienated from monoracial curricula, student groups, and student services, which reflect the monoracial categories and racial politics of the 1960s and 70s.

In the spirit of the historic Civil Rights Movement, which gave rise to the original ethnic studies centers, and in response to the predominance of mono-identity paradigms and institutional university structures, multiracial students at UCLA have begun a sustained project of community organizing and political empowerment. Multiethnic students have begun to organize themselves through the formation of the Mixed Student Union. In "Reflections on Mixed Heritage Student Community Building at UCLA," Camila Lacques documents the process of founding the Mixed Student Union at UCLA. In her words, "I quickly realized that the reality of where I came from did not formally exist at UCLA. I felt neither here nor there, not fully committed in my heart to any space because pieces of me were scattered about and I was seeking to feel whole. I teamed up with a friend of mine, Tara Sweatt, and we started devising plans to create a Mixed Student Union at UCLA (MSU) to help meet our personal needs as mixed students on campus." In this essay, Lacques honestly describes the challenges faced as part of the establishment of the MSU, including criticism and backlash from mono-identity student groups and a lack of historical racial consciousness among some students of mixed race ancestry. She also discusses various approaches for facilitating and building a safe space for mixed heritage students, and how to leverage mixed race collective identity as a political tool for action and change.

Building upon the narrative of the founding of the MSU at UCLA, editor Jenifer Logia reflects upon why multiethnic community organizing among college campuses is needed on a national level, and provides specific recommendations as to best practices. With great prescience, Logia declares: "Multiethnic community organizing on college campuses is crucial because multiethnic students have specific needs and experiences that are not always addressed by the university, in the classroom, in other ethnic/cultural student groups, or other aspects of college life (e.g., social life)... Beyond creating a safe space for dialogue, multiethnic student groups can work with university administrators to reform the way that race is counted and represented, reform the structure of academic programs to be more inclusive to multiethnic students and faculty, and advocate for more resources and programs that address the specific needs of multiethnic students."

As detailed by Ariel Pezner and Jenifer Logia in the third essay of this collection, the MSU's first major campus-wide action involved the implementation of the UCLA Multiethnic Diversity Pilot Survey. As a means of addressing the recent rise in hate speech and racist actions towards students of color, in 2014, UCLA administration officials conducted a university-wide "Campus Climate Survey." Unfortunately, despite its overall comprehensiveness, mixed race students were not recognized as a formal population in the survey, and their experience was therefore not considered. In response, MSU president Jenifer Logia created a student committee charged with the development and implementation of a sophisticated pilot survey which would evaluate campus climate for multiethnic students at UCLA. This committee also included Asian American studies graduate student, James Ong.

The results of the 2014 UCLA Multiethnic Diversity Pilot Survey were disheartening. A central finding was that multiethnic students are not included or acknowledged by UCLA as a discrete cultural population, and that an underlying sense of unwelcome pervades the experience of mixed race students in various campus groups. In the words of one student, "I feel as though there isn't really a place for mixed race people." Students also reported great discomfort in expressing their multiethnic identities in "the classroom" and in "Greek life (fraternities, sororities, professional, etc.)." In the blunt honesty of another student, "People stigmatize you as a minority and say things like 'Blacks, Mexicans, and mixed race people only got into UCLA because of affirmative action.'"

The report also revealed a dearth of curricular offerings related to the history and experience of mixed race peoples. Although a few meaningful mixed race courses have been offered through the department of Asian American studies under the sponsorship of Professor Lane Hirabayashi, such courses are few and far between on the broader UCLA campus. According to Pezner and Logia, "Often, the history of mixed race people is left out of textbooks and course readings, and therefore many of the classes revolving around race do not address the topic of mixed race. Attempts to create courses at UCLA that focus on mixed heritage and multiracial identity are challenging due to the lack of an appropriate department because they generally do not fit just one (e.g., Chicana/o studies, Asian American studies, or African American studies)."

Based upon the findings of the survey, the MSU proffers a number of specific recommendations aimed at improving campus climate for the growing mixed race student population. Acknowledging the limitations of its own study, which was based upon a sampling of twenty-eight students, the MSU recommends the design and implementation of a more comprehensive survey of multiethnic students, perhaps as part of the annual Campus Climate survey conducted by UCLA administration. This would engender the formal recognition of mixed race students as a discrete cultural population of the UCLA campus, as well as generate a clear picture of campus climate conditions for mixed race students leading to more comprehensive reforms.

The most powerful recommendation made by MSU student leaders is for the creation of a UCLA multiethnic studies center and a related degree in multiethnic studies. The UCLA multiethnic studies center would host an academic community for mixed race students and faculty at UCLA, and, as the first of its kind, would serve as a central institution for the advancement of mixed race studies in the nation. Furthermore, in the language of Pezner and Logia, it would also result in the "solidification of multiracial people as a unique ethnic group on campus and in academia." In sum, the first three essays of this collection articulate a nascent politics of mixed race at UCLA and evidence the rise of a unique third wave of the historic mixed race movement in the United States.

As further expressions of the developing multiethnic student movement at UCLA, the remaining essays offer theoretical explorations of the multiethnic experience in the United States, as well as personal reflections upon being mixed race. Drawing upon a wide range of cutting edge cultural theory, including critical race theory, post-structuralist theory, and Kristen Renn's ecology model of multiraciality, graduate student Lisa Yamasaki investigates the identity conflicts of some Latina/os whose phenotypical racial ambiguity allows for racial invisibility. In, "On Being Mixed Race in a *Mestizo*-Dominated Community," Emilie Santos Tumale explores the racial identity and consciousness of multiethnic Filipinos using Kevin Nadal's Filipino racial and ethnic identity development model, as well as the analytical frameworks of Christine Ijima Hall and Cynthia Nakashima.

It is significant to note that, although Tumale does not personally identify as mixed race, her important theoretical contribution is welcomed by the multiethnic student movement at UCLA and the mixed race editors of this collection. As discussed in the essay of Camila Lacques, it is imperative for the mixed heritage student community to build connections with, and seek the perspective of, mono-identity allies and student groups. In her words, "MSU can only thrive if we work well with the various communities that make up the collective mixedness that we are. We are only as strong as the parts of ourselves; we are only as unified as each member is unified within themselves." To this end, the mixed race student movement welcomes the theoretical and methodological insights, as well as political solidarity, of its mono-identity allies.

To conclude Part II, Jimmy Fang examines the social marginalization and identity struggles of "mekas dawb," or "blonde Hmongs." Fang's essay forces readers to grapple with how deeply phenotype shapes race relations in the United States, irrespective of culture, law, and even mono-ethnic community membership.

The final eight student contributions explore the mixed race student journey on a more personal level. In his essay, "Versions of Myself," editor James Ong reflects upon his own multiethnic Asian American identity, and describes his journey of being an outsider connected to multiple identities. In the poem, "Beautiful as Any Other," Cristal Maria Plantt muses upon her multiethnic experience utilizing the vivid imagery of multi-colored paints on a canvas. As a reflection of the cultural and geographical diversity represented in this anthology, Kathryn Loutzenheiser, Sophia Cole, and Molly Montgomery ponder their variegated experiences growing up Mexican and German, Black and Japanese, as well as Chinese/Irish/German/Scottish/French, in the three distinct locales of Hollywood, South Central, and the San Francisco Bay Area. In the following essays, "Listed as Other" and "Congratulations, You Look Like Me," Chinese hapas Leonard Haller and Aislinn Dunne reflect upon their multiracial lives through the lens of food and Eurocentric standards of beauty. In the concluding essay, titled, "Finding Lenses For My Myopic Green-Tinted Almond Eyes: My First Year as a Teaching Assistant," graduate student Emily H.A. Yen complicates the traditional mixed race narrative by examining the hitherto minimally explored intersectionality of multiethnicity and physical disability.

Notes

1   See Robert Chao Romero, *The Chinese in Mexico, 1882-1940* (Tucson: University of Arizona Press, 2010)

2   For more theological ruminations on mixed race identity, see Robert Chao Romero, *Jesus for Revolutionaries: An Introduction to Race, Social Justice, and Christianity*. (Los Angeles: Christian Ethnic Studies Press, 2013).

3   Chelsea Guillermo-Wann (2013), [Mixed] Race matters: Racial theory, Classification, and Campus Climate, (PhD diss., UCLA).

4   This book makes a modest contribution to the developing literature on mixed race university students. Kristen A. Renn pioneered this field of study with her seminal publication, *Mixed Race Students in College: The Ecology of Race, Identity, and Community on Campus* (Albany: State University of New York Press, 2004). *Being Mixed Race at UCLA* also builds upon the important recent publication by Andrew Garrod, Robert Kilkenny, and Christina Gómez titled, *Mixed: Multiracial College Students Tell Their Life Stories* (Ithaca: Cornell University Press, 2013). Focused upon the theme of multiethnic identity, *Mixed* presents the memoirs of 12 mixed race university students at Dartmouth College. Finally, this volume is also indebted to the path-breaking social scientific research of M.A. Kamimura, Chelsea Guillermo Wann, and Marc P. Johnston (See Kamimura 2010), Multiracial college students: Understanding interpersonal self- concept in the first year (PhD diss., University of Michigan); Wann (2013), [Mixed] Race matters: Racial theory, classification, and campus climate, (PhD diss., UCLA); and Johnston (2013), What's the use of race? Investigating the concept of race in higher education (PhD diss., UCLA)).

5   Scholars typically frame the multiracial movement in two waves—the first occurring in the 1990s, and the second in the 2000s.

6   See William H. Frey, *Diversity Explosion: How New Racial Demographics are Remaking America* (Washington DC: Brookings Institution, 2014), 205.

7   See United States Census Bureau (2012, Dec 12), U.S. Census Bureau projections show a slower growing, older, more diverse nation a half century from now. Retrieved from https://www.census.gov/newsroom/releases/archives/population/cb12-243.html; See also Cárdenas, V., Ajinkya, J. & and Gibbs Léger, D. (2011, Oct). Progress 2050: New Ideas for a Diverse America, *Center for American Progress*. Retrieved from https://www.americanprogress.org/wp content/uploads/issues/2011/10/pdf/progress_2050.pdf

8   William H. Frey, *Diversity Explosion* (Washington DC: Brookings Institution, 2014), 4.

9   United States Census Bureau (2010, Sept 27). 2010 census shows multiple-race population grew faster than two or more races population. Retrieved from https://www.census.gov/prod/cen2010/briefs/c2010br-13.pdf.

10 United States Census Bureau (2010). The two or more races population: 2010. Metro region/number of persons, two or more races/percentage of the total population. Retrieved from http://www.city-data.com/forum/city-vs-city/14 14333-cities-most-mixed-biracial-multiracial-people-2.html.

11 Wendy Wang, *The Rise of Intermarriage.* Pew Research Center, 2016. Retrieved from http://www.pewsocialtrends.org/2012/02/16/the-rise-of-intermarriage/. See also William H. Frey, *Diversity Explosion* (Washington DC: Brookings Institution, 2014), 195.

12 See United States Census Bureau (2010). The two or more races population: 2010.

13 Homi K. Bhabha, *The Location of Culture* (New York: Routledge, 1994).

14 With limited exception, the various ethnic studies centers at UCLA have been slow to incorporate mixed race literature into their programs of teaching and research. Within the canon of Asian American studies, important publications on the mixed race experience include: Maria P. P. Root, *Racially Mixed People in America* (Thousand Oaks: Sage Publications, 1992); Maria P. P. Root, *The Multiracial Experience* (Thousand Oaks: Sage Publications, 1995); Teresa Williams-León and Cynthia L. Nakashima, *The Sum of Our Parts: Mixed Heritage Asian Americans* (Philadelphia: Temple University Press, 2001); and Stephen L. H. Murphy-Shigematsu, *When Half is Whole: Asian American Identities (Stanford: Stanford University Press,* 2012). Another notable mixed race publication in Asian American Studies is the 1997 special edition of *The Amerasia Journal* titled, *No Passing Zone.*

In Chicana/o and Latina/o studies, the seminal mixed race publication is Rudy Guevarra's (2012) *Becoming Mexipino: Multiethnic identities and communities in San Diego.* New Brunswick: Rutgers. *Becoming Mexipino* tells the history of the mixed race Filipino-Mexican community of San Diego throughout the scope of the twentieth century. Other works encompassing the mixed race Latina/o experience include: Julia M. Schiavone-Camacho, *Chinese Mexicans: Transpacific Migration and the Search for a Homeland, 1910–1960 (*Chapel Hill: University of North Carolina Press, 2012); Grace Peña Delgado, *Making the Chinese Mexican: Global Migration, Localism, and Exclusion in the US-Mexico Borderlands* (Stanford: Stanford University Press, 2012); and Robert Chao Romero, *The Chinese in Mexico, 1882-1940* (Tucson: University of Arizona Press, 2010).

The mixed race literature in African American studies is by far the most developed. G. Reginald Daniel pioneered the field with his landmark (2001) publication, *More than Black: Multiracial Identity and the New Racial Order.* Philadelphia: Temple University Press. Other key scholars of the Black multiracial experience include: Sika Dagbovie-Mullins, *Crossing Black: Mixed-Race Identity in Modern American Fiction and Culture* (Knoxville: University of Tennessee Press, 2013); and Streeter, C. *Tragic No More: Mixed-Race Women and the Nexus of Sex and Celebrity* (Amherst: University of Massachusetts Press, 2012).

With respect to Native Americans, Arica L. Coleman, Andrew Jolivette, Tia Miles, and James Brooks have developed a solid corpus of research on the topic of Black-Indian relations and racial intermarriage over the past decade. See Arica L. Coleman, *That the Blood Stay Pure: African Americans, Native Americans and the Predicament of Race and Identity in Virginia* (Bloomington: Indiana University Press, 2013); Andrew Jolivette, *Louisiana Creoles: Cultural Recovery and Mixed-Race Native American Identity* (Lanham: Lexington Books, 2007); Tia Miles, *Ties That Bind: The Story of an Afro-Cherokee Family in Slavery and Freedom* (Berkeley: University of California Press, 2005); James Brooks, *Confounding the Color Line: The Indian-Black Experience in North America* (Lincoln: University of Nebraska Press, 2002). Also unique among the mixed-race historiography is the spiritual reflection offered by Frank E. Robinson, Jr., *Letters to a Mixed Race Son* (Create Space, 2012), and the creative Afro-Asian explorations of Janet Stickmon, *Crushing Soft Rubies: A Memoir* (Broken Shackle Publishing, 2003).

Part I: A Student Politics of Mixed Race

Reflections on Mixed Heritage Student Community Building at UCLA

Camila Lacques

The purpose of this essay is to document some of the thought processes behind building a mixed heritage community at UCLA, to demonstrate the unknown realities that we face as a community, and how intricate and complex mixed spaces can be. Also, the point is to help generate ideas for other college campuses, or other communities at UCLA, about how to build off of the work of others and pass on knowledge and skills between student organizers. While my reflections will reference the collective that built the space that I will be reflecting on, the work and ideas will be personal ones that I specifically gathered along my journey. It is not my intention to write on behalf of all of the founding members of MSU, rather speak to my personal experiences because each of us has our own perspectives on any given theme concerning the mixed heritage community.

The fall of 2010 was the start of my second year at UCLA and I was in limbo. As a woman of color coming from a low-income, first generation college student background, "fitting in" at UCLA did not come easy most of the time, as I tried to make my way through a university that was made up of largely middle class students and people who did not look like me. One of my biggest struggles was finding a community that was as mixed, diverse, and understanding of multiple identities as I was. I quickly realized that the reality of where I came from did not formally exist at UCLA. I felt neither here nor there, not fully committed in my heart to any space because pieces of me were scattered about. Seeking to feel whole, I teamed up with a friend of mine, Tara Sweatt, and we started devising plans to create a Mixed Student Union at UCLA (MSU) to help meet our personal needs as mixed students on campus. This reflection piece is broken up into three major parts concerning this process: (1) the challenges we faced establishing MSU, (2) effective approaches facilitating and building a safe space for mixed heritage students, and (3) tools we developed to politicize mixed heritage students.

The Challenges of Starting a Mixed Heritage Organization

Immediately after we founded the Mixed Student Union and starting outreaching to other people to get involved, I had many moments of realizations. For one, I quickly came to understand that even uttering the words, "mixed people" sparked conversations, confusion and questions all around. Even "mixed" people were puzzled by us, because they had simply never heard of mixed heritage people organizing together around their identities. We were bringing fresh ideas to a campus that has a long history of student organizations that have decades of experience, networks and alumni. We started as two people and grew to six people strong and were making every word up as we went. I was unsure of everything except the fact that a space for us was needed. The lack of consciousness, education and visibility of mixed heritage people overall on campus was shocking, frustrating and served as a road block when people even asked, "What is mixed?" We were met with curiosity but also moments of animosity because people do not always appreciate being challenged to think and understand the world in new ways outside of rigid social constructions of "Black and white." We do not fit into neat boxes, we exist outside of the obvious and push the envelope of identity by just being. The key to addressing the ignorance surrounding mixed peoples' existence is to take it as an opportunity and use it more as a force of motivation. The lack of mixed heritage presence on campus meant that we had the opportunity to create images, to construct ideas and to share our experiences in order to shape our campus' understanding of our families and histories. As long as there is a strong internal family within the organization, the collective potential is infinite.

An important first step for us was to get down to the basics: research. I searched for resources about mixed heritage history, novels, and articles, in order to build my own language so I could educate others about mixed heritage experiences. A general vocabulary is very helpful for articulating a wide range of themes within a given community. Then, step one: express to folks that mixed people in no way, shape or form have a homogenous set of life experiences nor do we all identify the same way, share the same politics, or even all care deeply about mixed heritage issues. It is a community unified in diversity that will always have deep chasms, differences and complexities just like any other community. By working on making the mixed heritage community more visible, we were putting ourselves out there to be vulnerable about our struggles with identity, racism, and even self-esteem, as well as expressing our positive and empowering realities as mixed people. This vulnerability was a challenge as it was faced with rejection and general disinterest by people on campus. It was important that we constantly checked in with one another and listened to one another as we shared stories of passing out fliers and engaging in conversation about mixed heritage people with the general UCLA population.

Much of the ignorance I encountered came in the form of jokes such as, "Oh I get it, the Mutt Student Union," or, "Oh, do you all sit around and talk about how confused you all are?" or vain comments like, "Oh, cool, yea, mixed babies are so cute! I support that!" I did not realize that there were commonly held myths about mixed people. For example, some people think that mixed people are always of European heritage and something else, or that mixed-ness only exists in the form of two races or ethnicities, and nothing more. Battling plain ignorance can be exhausting and because of that, it is important, as I mentioned above, to create a strong family within the leadership of a mixed heritage organization in order to collectively prepare for rejection and misunderstanding. Our leadership was able to build trust and love in a way that gave us all the confidence to speak openly and courageously with others on campus and our strong collective presence forced people to take us seriously. Our intention to create MSU for the sake of our well being was impossible to attack at a certain point because we worked so hard to normalize our existence and our collective diverse identity.

Establishing ourselves on campus, however, did require more than just conversations with individuals; it also forced us to establish relationships with existing monocultural, ethnic, racial and political groups on campus.

Each university is unique and at UCLA there is a rich tradition of identity-based student organizing that is the backbone of students of color community building on campus. One of the most imperative connections to build mixed heritage student spaces is with already established identity-based organizations. We, as MSU at UCLA, faced some criticism and minor backlash for our very existence from certain identity-based spaces or involved students because there was a lack of understanding of the purpose of MSU at UCLA. We were seen as a potential threat to other spaces in the sense that we were also outreaching to students of color and specifically because we were targeting students that were not already active in identity-based spaces due to their discomfort, for example. As soon as we were made aware that there was concern regarding our outreach and efforts as an organization, we sat down to have dialogue with leadership from other groups in order to articulate our needs and purpose and how we aimed to work closely with mono-identity based groups in the future. MSU can only thrive if we work well with the various communities that make up the collective mixed-ness that we are. We are only as strong as the parts of ourselves; we are only as unified as each member is unified within themselves.

One key lesson I took away from the dialogue we had with mono-identity groups was that some members and leadership within MSU were unaware of the histories and conditions of certain communities. Mixed-ness in some communities and families in particular, depending on their history, can be seen as a good thing and others view mixed-ness as betrayal to one's community. Some of the issues we needed to revisit were ideas of colorism, racism, white supremacy and colonization in order to try and contextualize some people's concern over MSU impeding on other communities' perceived membership. At the end of the day, members of MSU are inherently part of mono-identity groups as they identify with their respective communities but at the same time can have ignorance, in some cases, to what mixed-ness is read as by certain people. Being pushed to the margins of a community can cause a break in understanding and lack of insight into certain cultural norms and experiences, sometimes leaving mixed heritage folks with a hole in their understandings of cultural expectations or commonly held beliefs. So, no, mixed people should not be ashamed nor hide their various identities, but yes, should most definitely be aware of the various narratives surrounding mixed-ness in their communities. For example, in my community as a Chicana, "mestizo" meaning "mixed person" in Spanish, can be associated with the legacy of rape from the genocide and colonization of indigenous land and people of the Americas on behalf of the Spanish. Speaking about mixed-ness is always rooted in historical experiences no matter who is in the conversation.

Some of the comments that were circulated included the following: "Oh, do they think they are too good to participate in our group?" "Do they not identify with this part of their heritage, are they ashamed?" These recurring and nightmarish comments questioned the very assumption that mixed heritage students need support and a safe space in the first space. Yes, some people do not feel comfortable in certain groups of people because someone is constantly commenting on their so-called lack of ethnic or cultural authenticity because they are mixed, or questioning their identity in general. It is an awful experience constantly being required to explain oneself to the world around you especially when mixed-ness is critiqued as a choice. There is no question that interracial, intercultural, and interethnic relationships all pose important questions about bias, prejudice, and preference but they also bring up issues of love, struggle, and openness. When all was said and done, we as MSU leadership were able to reach out and listen to people's concerns while not letting our sensitivities or egos get in the way, and were able to firmly establish our need to collectively organize while gaining allies in the process. Being open, honest, and willing to listen, learn and share with others will always ultimately pay off in the process of campus community building. MSU today is more effective because of mono-identity groups, their resources and outreach and now, mono-identity groups have tools and support to refer to for mixed heritage students within their communities.

Creating Safe Spaces for Mixed Heritage Students

Once we created an organization, built a leadership, and had a growing membership, we had to create tools and a culture within the organization that was supportive, comforting and safe, while also making room for disagreement and growth. Given that every MSU participant was drawn to the organization for different reasons, we could not generalize our membership. There was no set consciousness surrounding history, or race, or intergroup dialogue established. We had to learn to meet each participant where they were at, from students who just wanted to make friends and had no interest in being political or speaking about identity at all, to students who deeply sought healing and education regarding their experience and the mixed heritage community at large. Judgment was not allowed. All students are on their own journey with their identity and how they view themselves in the world, thus it is impractical and harmful to force an identity or a type of thinking onto someone. We surveyed the membership to see what issues were most important to them and made sure to have a wide range of topics open for discussion.

One exercise we were loyal to was creating "Statements of Unity." These statements were agreed upon and devised collectively in order to direct the intentions of the space, and the ways in which we wanted to conduct ourselves as an always evolving organization. One example of these Statements of Unity was to "Check our Privileges," which is a reminder to everyone in the space that even though we share a common identity as mixed heritage people, we each carry with us distinct experiences based on our gender, color, socioeconomic background, and sexuality, among many other factors. We all walk into MSU with privileges and struggles that must be confronted as we aim to dismantle oppression and question hierarchical power dynamics overall. There is no way to speak about mixed-ness without addressing queer identities and what role hetero-normativity plays in different cultures. We cannot speak about racism without talking about patriarchy and the experiences of female-identified members in our space. No societal reality is off limits or non-existent in any student organization. By acknowledging power, privilege and oppression, we helped create a political dialogue based on intersectionality while always aiming to protect each person's expression and well being.

A safe space for us also meant collective growth and widening of our understandings of what mixed-ness is and what it can mean. In order for all mixed heritage students to feel like they had a home in MSU we had to challenge what traditional ideas of "mixed" means and broaden the realities, for example that mixed-ness exists in the form of transracial adoptive families and multinational upbringings. The commonly held perception that mixed people fall into biracial identities and are typically mixed with Black and white constricts the true lengths of mixed heritage experiences. So, empathetic approaches of going beyond surface level substance in our space helped us get to know one another to the point where trust could be gained and assumptions are not welcomed. Mixedness is so broad and so unique and specific to each person that each participant brings new lessons and a new perspective for everyone. There is a careful line to walk between respect of one another's experiences and the need to be politically conscious and empathetic of the language and way we carry ourselves in the space.

One huge way that we created safety and a security blanket for our collective was building relationships with community based organizations. In our first year of MSU we linked up with MASC, Multiracial Americans of Southern California. Our relationship was a coming together of generations as we aimed to lean on MASC for support and guidance as we pushed to develop MSU. We co-programmed and shared resources with one another in order to bring the two spaces together. We had access to free space and they had access to funding that we had no budget for. The same reality exists in any collaboration; everyone has something unique to offer. There is an innate strength in the coming together of different groups because there is always the possibility of something completely new being born. The number one lesson I took away from our space-building process is to never assume and always listen to everyone around you when you are facilitating because you can always try to anticipate conflict and moments of learning in such a diverse group and see them through. A safe space is one in which people feel brave enough to be themselves, speak their minds, and be courageous enough to grow.

Politicizing Mixed Heritage Students

Beyond establishing ourselves on campus, we as MSU leadership aimed to not only create a family for mixed heritage students, but also to use our collective identity as a political tool for action and change. Purely social clubs serve a distinct purpose, but MSU had the potential to be something more; we had the potential to use our voices and identity for radical expression and to utilize our understanding of different types of oppression to politically align ourselves. One of my personal goals was to help make MSU an advocacy space not only for people of mixed heritage, but to take strong stands against racism, white supremacy, homophobia and sexism for example, because ultimately all struggles are connected. To understand the political implications of mixed heritage people, we have to recognize and/or tell our stories. Naming our families' journeys, struggles, triumphs, migrations and unique paths helps to paint a picture of what each person carries within them. An activity that we often started off meetings or workshops with was an exercise called "Mapping our Migration Stories." Each person would illustrate their several families' histories through images, maps, colors, and words. This exercise gives students a space to express themselves and their intricate or charged ancestral background through an artistic outlet that takes the pressure off the individual and puts the attention on the images that they create. Telling our stories, to share what brought our families together across generations, or what tore them apart, is a way to claim who we are and where we come from. To understand our families is to understand the impossibilities of our existence and at the same time, the normalcy in which we carry our pasts within us all the time. Every story is political in that it reveals tension, reasons people migrate or flee from their homes, and why and where they encounter people of other racial, cultural or ethnic backgrounds. I always aimed to emphasize that every self-identified mixed person is inherently political in that we exist in a system that at many points in history forbade the mixing of religions or races either institutionally or informally. To name our shared and distinct truths as a collective gives us historical context in which we can situate our understanding of identity and struggle overall.

Providing a space for students to share the good, the bad and the ugly of their pasts also opens a space up to discuss certain issues and compare experiences and exchange stories. A lot of our bonding as a collective stemmed from laughing and crying together noticing that we had experienced similar joy and pain. A dialogue between students with roots stemming from all over the world, with all kinds of different colors, hair colors, names, that speak several different languages and proudly claim unique identities, is by definition a political act. In my personal experience, the most intense learning I had came from moments of disagreements. Some students showed up to MSU just by chance or curiosity and had no prior experiences speaking about their mixed-ness or even gave any attention to it. Therefore, our discussions involved an incredible array of opinions and perspectives. Ignorance surrounding race and identity does not only exist on behalf of white people; ignorance exists in all communities regarding other communities and struggles. MSU and its members are no stranger to the learning process because educating ourselves is critical to the daily reality of coalition building. Some MSU members came from very privileged two-parent households, while others came from low-income single parent households. Some came from conservative small towns and others from racially segregated cities.

The incredible diversity in our organization made room for serious dialogue and disagreement. The politicization of MSU in part, was due to the fact that we literally had to educate one another on each other's experiences. The one certainty that each person holds onto in MSU is that they are the owners and experts of their personal experiences. Outside of oneself, no has the authority over any one topic or issue. One crucial topic in the mixed heritage community that always brought up critical discussion and contrasting opinions was the debate surrounding trans-racial adoption. We chose to never shy away from a topic, or be scared to voice our thoughts on very charged issues including whether or not it was socially/racially conscious or responsible for children of color to be adopted by white families. Trans-racial adoption is more and more common and often exists in an international context where more developed countries are adopting children internationally from poorer countries. Several MSU members brought up different perspectives throughout our conversations including opinions regarding class, sexuality, white privilege, and ideas of a post-racial United States society. Ultimately, a mixed heritage space cannot exist as a political force without explicit political conversations that get to the heart of questions about power, racism, colorism, and privilege. With these conversations come disagreement, frustration, challenging experiences, and hopefully, growth and education.

Another crucial step in building a politically conscious and active core membership would be to rally members around central mixed heritage issues or events. At UCLA we focused on celebrating Loving Day and getting mixed heritage students on campus to sign up for bone marrow registration. Loving Day is celebrated mid-June every year to mark the 1967 United States Supreme Court case that struck down anti-miscegenation laws in the United States. Loving Day is a part of the collective mixed heritage experience in the United States because it addresses the reality of the community existing as a whole. More specifically, because the Loving v. Virginia case involved an African American woman and a white American man fighting to legally marry, it is a moment for the mixed heritage community to deeper understand the roots of anti-miscegenation in the United States context of white supremacy and anti-Black racism. In addition, MSU at UCLA organized bringing Mixed Marrow, a community organization, to campus to attend our panels or events to outreach to multiethnic students specifically. Mixed Marrow aims to specifically recruit multiethnic people to sign up for a bone marrow registry. Multiethnic patients have a lower chance of finding a bone marrow match given the link between bone marrow and geographical and ethnic origins. This is an issue that explicitly and directly addresses a need in our community that can be easily supported. It is essential to connect members of the community to causes and shared meaningful goals in order to build a sense of connectedness and solidarity surrounding collective issues and history.

Lastly, the most powerful tool for politicizing mixed heritage students in my experience was the practice and protection of the right for one to self-identify. Personal identification is an extraordinarily political act because it allows people to decide for themselves, according to their own self-reflection and experiences, how they see and position themselves in society and where society sees and positions them. MSU at UCLA was founded on the idea that any member can identify as they choose; in our space people were not going to be assumed to racially/ethnically/linguistically/religiously/culturally identify a certain way. We were not going to judge or pry our way into each person's background. Members were open to express themselves how and when they chose. I drew inspiration from Maria P. Roots' work titled, the "Bill of Rights for Mixed People," in which she lays out several empowering and inclusive rights of mixed-identified people (Root 1996). This resource is a great starting point for speaking about self-identification and the various experiences of mixed people throughout their lives, amongst different families, and within their immediate families. Here is the full length of Roots', "Bill of Rights for People of Mixed Heritage"(Root 1996):

I HAVE THE RIGHT...

Not to justify my existence in this world.

Not to keep the races separate within me.

Not to justify my ethnic legitimacy.

Not to be responsible for people's discomfort with my physical or ethnic ambiguity.

I HAVE THE RIGHT...

To identify myself differently than strangers expect me to identify.

To identify myself differently than how my parents identify me.

To identify myself differently than my brothers and sisters.

To identify myself differently in different situations.

I HAVE THE RIGHT...

To create a vocabulary to communicate about being multiracial or multiethnic.

To change my identity over my lifetime--and more than once.

To have loyalties and identification with more than one group of people.

To freely choose whom I befriend and love

Bibliography

Root, Maria P.P. *The Multiracial Experience: Racial Borders as the New Frontier.* Thousand Oaks, CA: Sage Publications, 1995.

Multiethnic Community Organizing on College Campuses

Jenifer Logia

After accepting my offer to attend UCLA, I was just as excited as anyone else to begin college life at one of the top universities in the country. As a high school student, I was involved with various clubs and extracurricular activities that instilled a passion for social justice from an early age. I wanted to continue this work in college and join student groups that gave me a sense of belonging in a school of over 30,000 students. However, in the midst of all the pamphlets and flyers that were sent to me in the mail, inviting me to join student groups that matched the various ethnicity boxes I had checked on my application, I was hesitant to join anything at all. As a multiethnic woman of Nicaraguan, Filipino, and Chamorro heritage, where would I fit in? I read up on student groups such as Movimiento Estudiantil Chicanx de Aztlan (MEChA), Samahang Pilipino, and the Pacific Islanders Student Association. While all of them interested me equally, I couldn't pick one over another if it meant determining my student life experience for the next four years.

My difficulty with choosing which student groups to join on campus is just one example of how university life is not organized in a way that is inclusive to students like me, who identify with more than one race, ethnicity, culture, or nationality. If I wanted to declare a major in ethnic studies, I had to choose between Chicana/o studies or Asian American studies. If I wanted to join a cultural sorority, I would have to choose between the Latina one or the Asian one. None of the themed halls in the freshmen dorms were inclusive to multiethnic students. Even scholarship applications were organized into racial categories. When I applied for my first part-time job on campus, I was asked to identify my ethnicity with clear instructions to "check one box only." During my first year of college, I quickly learned that in order to navigate academic and social life at UCLA, I either had to identify with only one side of my heritage, or simply avoid getting involved in any cultural activities.

My attempts to find a sense of belonging was challenging at first, but I eventually found a student group called Mixed Student Union (MSU). When I came across this group as a freshman, it had only existed for about one year, the membership was small, and not many people had heard of it. However, I was instantly drawn to the group and began to feel that sense of belonging I was searching for. It was the first time in my life that I had heard of a space specifically meant for people of multiple racial or ethnic identities. In fact, it was the first time I had ever considered that people of mixed race could identify as a community and organize for their own unique needs. At the first meeting I attended, I met students with all sorts of different blends of cultures and heritages: Black and Korean, British and Ecuadorean, Mexican and Native American roots, and many more. I was in a room of people that made me feel comfortable enough to share that I was Latina, Asian and Pacific Islander without judgment or question. Being exposed to this group was transformative and powerful; it completely changed the way I understood my own identity and where I could fit in at UCLA. I had finally found a place where I truly felt I belonged.

In addition to my involvement with MSU, I was also fortunate enough to take a number of academic courses that allowed me to learn about the history of multiethnic people and the political implications of multiethnic identity. Through my campus organizing and academic coursework, I was able to learn from graduate students, professors, scholars, authors, and community leaders from the greater Los Angeles area and across California who dedicated their work to serving multiethnic communities. I look back at those experiences as pivotal in shaping the person and leader I've become.

I now take this opportunity to reflect on what I learned after being involved in MSU, as an active member for two years and as director for two years. In this essay, I will outline reasons why I believe multiethnic community building is needed on college campuses, and describe some of the shortcomings within administrative research and publications, academic coursework, student groups, and other areas of student life that are not inclusive to multiethnic students. Secondly, I will provide personal examples from my own multiethnic organizing efforts to illustrate the positive benefits of having a strong multiethnic community on campus. And lastly, I will offer recommendations of how multiethnic community organizing on college campuses can improve and continue to grow, and suggest some tangible goals that multiethnic college students can work towards in the near future. For multiethnic students, reclaiming a sense of one's own identity can help build the confidence needed to get involved on a wider array of campus issues.

The Need for Multiethnic Community Organizing on College Campuses

College students have a long history of organizing social movements to demand a quality education and take a stand on various social issues. At every university, there are a number of student groups and student leaders who advocate on behalf of minority groups; however, there seems to be a lack of student activism towards multiethnic students specifically. In my own experience of trying to build a platform for multiethnic students at UCLA, I've had people ask me a variety of questions as to why multiethnic students need a group of their own. Some people feel that a multiethnic student group would take away from other ethnic student groups that already exist. Others believe that being multiracial is a positive trait, and that multiracial students actually have an advantage because they are able to identify with multiple groups. However, I argue that there are many reasons why multiethnic community organizing and student activism is needed on college campuses.

First, multiethnic students are not represented in diversity-related research and publications that come from the administrative level. For instance, universities often show demographic profiles that reflect the ethnic makeup of their student population, but when I look at these charts and graphs, I question how people like me fit into these models. With traditional racial categories, multiethnic students are either misrepresented or erased from demographic data sets. If those numbers are used to make decisions on how to best serve students, then administrators must begin to collect data in a way that accurately captures the multiethnic population. As multiethnic community organizing continues to grow, administrators may begin to see the value in changing the ways that demographic data is collected.

A second reason why multiethnic community organizing is needed on college campuses is to ensure that students receive the quality education they deserve. At many universities such as UCLA, ethnic studies departments are separated into traditional racial categories: African American studies, Asian American studies, Chicana/o studies, and American Indian studies. Organizing academic departments in this way can be limiting and doesn't reflect the way that race is experienced by many people. Multiethnic students should have the opportunity to learn about their own identity and the history of multiethnic peoples. Although multiethnic studies has a strong and ever-growing presence in academia, no university in the country offers a multiethnic studies center, department, major, minor, or any type of academic program. Some universities offer individual courses with topics related to mixed race people and history, however, they are scattered across departments and students who are interested in multiethnic studies have no centralized means of getting the few resources that do exist. Moreover, students would have little reason to take these courses (other than for personal interest) unless they were integrated into an academic program or fulfilled a general education requirement. Multiethnic student organizers can take these shortcomings as opportunities to advocate for change within academic departments, and improve the overall quality of education that the university offers.

Lastly, multiethnic community organizing is needed on college campuses to work towards making student life (outside of academic life) more inclusive to multiethnic people. Many college campuses still do not have student groups or clubs dedicated to those who identify as multiethnic. Universities like UCLA have a number of culturally specific outreach, retention, and access programs, yet it is difficult for multiethnic students to use these resources due to the way they are categorized by race/ethnicity. Other aspects of student life outside of student activism are organized by traditional racial categories, including but not limited to: cultural fraternities and sororities, culturally themed freshmen dorms, welcome programs for admitted freshmen and transfer students, scholarships for specific cultural groups, alumni networks of ethnic and cultural groups, cultural shows and performances, programming that celebrate cultural history, student conferences, and more.

A student's racial identity sets the foundation for his or her entire college experience. When you identify as multiethnic and do not quite fit in to any one category, it is easy to feel lost, excluded, and frustrated when trying to navigate through the university every day. When you understand how important racial identity is to determining one's student experience, it becomes easier to understand why multiethnic community organizing is needed on college campuses.

Outcomes of Multiethnic Community Organizing: Personal Experiences from UCLA

In my experiences with MSU, I've seen the wide range of benefits that come from community building for multiethnic students. These benefits are not only limited to the on-campus experience, but help strengthen the multiethnic community long after graduation. I hope that my personal anecdotes can serve as examples of how multiethnic students can be an integral part of a diverse student body and the wider community.

One of the first benefits that come from organizing a space for multiethnic students is having the opportunity to transform the way students think about their personal identity, often for the first time. Most multiethnic students do not have clubs in high school or extracurricular activities that focus on multiethnic identity, so college can be a very important time for young students to develop the way that they see themselves. I especially enjoyed talking to first year students and recruiting new members to join MSU because something new always sparked in their minds when having such personal conversations.

The conversations and dialogue that took place at our weekly meetings and social events were the backbone of what made MSU a success. Throughout the course of the year, we held meetings that facilitated critical discussions of multiracial identity, history, microaggressions, intersectionality, representations of mixed race people in the media, family dynamics, affirmative action policies, ideas of beauty, interracial dating and relationships, race and medicine, and much more. These meetings were student planned and executed, and took place in a simple classroom setting that allowed for organic and free-flowing exchange of thoughts. We challenged each other to think about how race operates in society, and talked about experiences that had affected us for our whole lives but were never put into words. Over time, students began to embrace their multiracial identities in ways they had never done before. The time spent engaged in these meetings were some of my most memorable and meaningful experiences I had in college, and the people I met through MSU became my closest friends.

The process of community building for multiethnic students did not only come from our weekly meetings and discussions on the UCLA campus. Our group was able to branch out across the University of California (UC) system and interact with students from universities across the nation. My first experience branching outside of my own university was taking a trip to the University of California Berkeley, where I attended their annual Mixed Student Union conference. Students from UC Berkeley, UCLA, UC Santa Cruz, UC Santa Barbara, UC Davis, and more attended this event. I was amazed to see that the multiethnic student experience was gaining such far-reaching attention. I was introduced to professors, graduate students, scholars, authors, and community members who focused their research and teaching on issues related to multiethnic identity. During my time as a student, I was able to attend a number of conferences in which students across the state were able to come together and talk about the specific issues that multiethnic students faced on their college campuses. One of my favorite experiences was being able to facilitate the multiracial student caucus at the 2013 Student of Color Conference. I was able to hear from hundreds of multiethnic students who discussed issues of racial microaggressions, lack of inclusivity from the university, lack of academic courses on multiracial topics, and how many campuses still did not have any student group, programs, or resources for multiethnic students. Being able to participate in these conferences and events helped to frame my work within a much broader context and motivated me to continue building a strong multiethnic community.

Lastly, another benefit that came from multiethnic community organizing at UCLA was connecting students to the multiethnic community outside of the university setting. Before getting involved in MSU, I had no idea that so many organizations existed for multiethnic people. MSU was able to connect more people to the greater multiethnic movement happening in Los Angeles and throughout California. MSU has developed a close relationship with the Multiracial Americans of Southern California (MASC), a community group for multiethnic individuals and mixed race families. In addition, MSU hosted bone marrow drives in conjunction with Mixed Marrow, an organization that aims to register multiethnic people as bone marrow donors. MSU also attended the grand opening of the Hapa exhibit at the Japanese American National Museum in Los Angeles, which was the first-ever historical museum exhibit focusing on the history of Hapa identity. Lastly, at our annual Mixed Heritage conference, we connected with even more multiethnic organizations, such as the Mixed Remixed Festival and the "100% Mixed Show" YouTube Channel. Through all of these interactions, we developed a mutually beneficial relationship with these organizations and community leaders, and together we helped to move the multiethnic community forward.

Recommendations for Future Multiethnic Student Organizing Campaigns

While the organizing efforts of MSU have helped to promote inclusivity and community-building for multiethnic college students, there is still plenty of room for growth. Students who are dedicated to strengthening the presence of multiethnic identity on college campuses should organize towards making changes on the academic and administrative levels of their universities, as well as continuing to increase the number of multiethnic student groups across the nation. I offer the following four recommendations for future multiethnic student organizing campaigns:

1. *Create a student group for multiethnic students on your campus*
One of the first things that multiethnic students can do to increase representation is to start a student group for multiethnic students if one does not already exist on campus. Reach out to other campuses that have well-established multiethnic student groups and ask for advice on how to start your own. It is important to establish a strong community base at the

grassroots level before organizing towards more challenging administrative changes.

2. *Work towards more resources and programming to address multiethnic student issues*

In addition to creating safe spaces for meetings, critical dialogue, and social events, students can create regular projects and events that will continue on an annual basis. Many mixed student groups on various campuses have come up with their own versions of such projects, including "Admit Day" programs for incoming freshmen and transfer students (UC Berkeley), Mixed Heritage Week celebration and series of events (UC Davis), Mixed Culture Show to celebrate multicultural dance, music, and art (UC Irvine), annual Mixed Heritage Conference to bring together scholars and community organizers from different regions (UC Berkeley and UCLA), bone marrow registration drives, historical museum exhibits, and more. These are a few examples of programs and events that have been successful at various college campuses that could be expanded upon at other schools. In addition, if your school hosts any diversity-related programs, make sure that multiethnic people are included in some way. If not, student groups can raise their voices to ensure that they are represented.

3. *Advocate for multiethnic representation in academics*

Multiethnic students can organize and advocate for more inclusive ethnic studies departments, cultural centers, academic programs, coursework, journals, publications, and research opportunities to include the histories of mixed race people and multiethnic identity in the United State and across the globe. Students can do research on which faculty members at their university focus on multiethnic studies, and work with them as allies to advocate for more culturally relevant courses. To date, no college campus in the United States offers a major or minor program in multiethnic studies. This is something that students could advocate for and achieve which has never been done before. The success of multiethnic community organizing on college campuses cannot reach its full potential without having an educational component to complement the activism. If student leaders have a better understanding of their own history, they will be better equipped to organize and foster a healthy community of multiethnic students.

4. *Demand the inclusion of multiethnic students in administrative research and publications*

A strong multiethnic student community base on college campuses would be able to pressure administrators to reform the way that race and ethnicity data is collected and used in research and publications. It is an injustice to multiethnic students to not be represented in campus research and publications that directly affect them. Universities should avoid publishing false data or presenting misleading information about the racial/ethnic makeup of its student body. There are alternative models that universities can start to use to better represent people of mixed race. Students should demand that universities change the way they ask about race and ethnicity on college applications, job applications, and survey questions. These changes will not only help multiethnic students, but also any other ethnic group who gets aggregated into umbrella racial categories.

A Discussion of Results and Recommendations from the 2014 UCLA Multiethnic Diversity Pilot Survey

Ariel Pezner and Jenifer Logia

In recent years, UCLA has experienced a number of incidents in which ethnic groups have been targeted through hateful speech and other actions, leading to high tensions among students at UCLA. In response to this increased strain and demands for the school to take action, UCLA conducted a university-wide campus climate survey in hopes of gaining a better understanding of race relations and prejudice at UCLA. However, despite the overwhelming length and detail of the campus climate survey, the survey failed to mention multiethnicity in any of its questions or answer options. Considering how much of an issue diversity has become at UCLA, it is unfortunate that students of mixed race were left out of this important discussion.

Despite UCLA administrators' lack of formal recognition of multiethnic students, this demographic still holds a strong presence on the UCLA campus. Mixed Student Union, a student-led group at UCLA, has existed since 2010 and has continually grown in size and influence. In addition, there are a number of courses offered on topics of multiracial identity and history, taught by faculty members who also identify as multiethnic. The multiethnic population at UCLA is a necessary and powerful force on campus, and the campus climate survey ignores a large group of students, faculty, and community members who play a very important role in UCLA's campus climate.

Purpose

To address the lack of inclusion from the campus climate survey, members of Mixed Student Union conducted their own survey to seek input from multiethnic students regarding how they feel about campus climate. The purpose of the survey was to account for the lack of multiethnic student voices in assessing campus climate, as well as views of the multiethnic climate by monoethnic students. The multiethnic population has a significant presence on campus, and the experiences of these students should be taken into account in campus-wide diversity efforts. The survey was designed to get an idea of what campus climate is like for multiethnic students, and bring to light some of the issues that multiethnic students face at UCLA. It is aimed at both dismantling many of the stereotypes and misconceptions that people have about multiethnic people in general, and allowing multiethnic students to tell their own stories and be heard.

Survey Methodology

The proposal to implement a survey regarding campus climate for students of multiracial or multiethnic backgrounds began as a part of UCLA's 2014 Diversity Symposium. The Mixed Student Union 2013-2014 President, Jenifer Logia, created a committee with five other Mixed Student Union members, as well as a UCLA graduate student in the Asian American studies department, to create and distribute the survey. Through a series of meetings and discussion, the committee developed the survey layout and questions as a Google Survey.

In order to get the most accurate and diverse responses, the questions were designed so that all students, whether they identify as multiethnic or not, could answer them. Because campus climate is something that students of any background can acknowledge and participate in, the committee wanted to make sure the survey was as inclusive as possible. The committee sought to understand how multiethnic students felt about campus climate, but also wanted to know how other students felt about campus climate for multiethnic students. Space was provided to allow the survey takers to expand on their answers and share personal anecdotes, which allowed for a wider interpretation of the responses.

Many of the questions were not required, in order to accommodate more survey takers, and, furthermore, the survey was created to have a short length of only ten questions to further motivate students to participate. Also included was a space to provide an email address if the survey taker would be willing to participate in an oral history project at a later date.

Committee members shared the link to the survey on Facebook, email, and other social media directly to UCLA students and faculty. The post was made visible only to those affiliated with UCLA, and it was made clear in the introduction to the survey that it was aimed at those who can accurately attest to the campus climate specifically at UCLA.

Demographics of Survey-Takers

Of the twenty-eight responses collected, about a fourth were from first-year students, over a third were from third-year students, and the remaining responses were from second and fourth year students, and one graduate student. The majors of the survey-takers covered a wide range, from the science and engineering to the humanities and social sciences. Of the twenty-eight responders, twenty-two self-identified as multiracial, multiethnic, or otherwise multicultural, and the other six self-identified as only one race or nationality.

Analysis of Survey Responses
Describing Campus Climate for Multiethnic Students

The first question of the survey asked participants to describe campus climate for multiethnic students. For many students, the answer to this question was that multiethnic students are not included or acknowledged by UCLA. For example, one student wrote, "I feel as though there isn't really a place for mixed race people." Another student explained with more detail that, "I don't think it's something that the average student thinks about. For the most part, mixed race kids are not viewed as mixed race, usually because society finds it easier to label them as one race. So multiethnic students become nonexistent." Some students felt that "the main problem on campus is the lack of clear representation of multiethnicity by the UCLA administration," and for this reason "often times multiethnic students are pressured into choosing one side over the other just to make it easier for themselves to navigate campus life."

Level of Comfort or Discomfort in Discussing Mixed Identity

One of the most influential determinants in campus climate is how students feel in the classroom, in residential halls, and in the activities they participate in. When asked where they feel most *comfortable* discussing and/or expressing multiethnic identity, the most popular responses were, first, "with peers" and second, in "ethnic or cultural student groups." When discussing personal topics like identity, race, culture, and ethnicity, it makes sense to feel most comfortable with friends or in spaces where the topic is already on the minds of the people. However, it is important to note that not every survey-taker marked both or either of these options. There were many responses expressing that their comfort in ethnic or cultural student groups was not consistent for all organizations, as one student states, "I am comfortable in certain cultural student groups but not others." Similarly, many people noted that they feel most comfortable discussing these topics with other mixed race people over those who were not, for fear of a lack of understanding.

When asked where they feel *uncomfortable* discussing and/or expressing multiethnic identity, the most popular selections were in "the classroom" and in "Greek life (fraternities, sororities, professional, etc.)." These responses are the most telling of what the campus climate is truly like for the discussion of culture and race. While the topics of race and culture may not be applicable to every classroom, students should still feel comfortable discussing these topics in an educational environment. However, it is clear that they do not feel able to do so. One student expresses, "These are awkward places to discuss race. People stigmatize you as a minority and say things like 'Blacks, Mexicans, and mixed race people only got into UCLA because of affirmative action.'"

Others echo the sentiments of this student's response: "I just think it's hard to explain in class about myself, not that I fear any judgment, I just don't want the attention." Most stated that they simply felt that certain locations were not "appropriate" places to discuss race. The few who stated that they are usually comfortable noted that their knowledge on the subject made them feel more confident in discussing their identity.

Similarly, the choice of "Greek life" is also revealing. In a group setting that is meant to create a strong bond among students ("brotherhood" or "sisterhood"), it would appear surprising that students do not feel comfortable discussing and/or expressing multiethnic identity. Many of the students explained this as fear of being stereotyped by what they reveal about themselves. One explains it as "simply because these folks minimize identity to be subjective and not an important issue."

Importance of Acknowledging Multiethnicity in Various Contexts

In order to help establish our survey goals, one of the first questions that the students answered was "Do you think acknowledging multiethnic identity (in class curriculums, demographic surveys, campus literature, research, etc.) is an important part of having a diverse campus?" The answers to this question help reveal more about respondents' views on multiethnicity, as well as their definition of diversity. The overwhelming majority (89 percent) of survey-takers responded with "yes." Many echoed similar sentiments such as: "You can't lump all mixed race people into monoracial categories," "it's especially important to bring more awareness to the fact that mixed race people exist and have a voice," "not acknowledging those identities is overlooking a person's identity as if their experiences do not exist or are not important," and more. Overall, most agreed that multiethnic students do not fit into one category, and most people who are not multiracial fail to see this, which limits the diversity of our campus.

However, one of the twenty-eight respondents checked "no." This student, who identified as a mixed race individual, stated, "I do not think UCLA has a diversity problem" and that acknowledging multiethnic identity on campus "will waste time and our money. If you really have to teach people here how to respect diversity in Los Angeles then they are a lost cause." While he or she is not particularly against acknowledging multiethnic identity on campus, this person has a pessimistic view of his or her peer's ability to learn more about diversity. This person claims that having to "teach" people diversity is a waste of time, which makes it seem as if this person expects students to come to UCLA completely open-minded, and that students have no ability to change mindsets.

Positive and Negative Experiences with having a Multiethnic Identity

Having a multiethnic identity, as with any identity, comes with both positive and negative experiences. In this part of the survey we wanted to see the balance of positive versus negative experiences related to having multiethnic identity, and hear some of the specific stories that students wanted to share. In both forms of the question, the majority of respondents had positive experiences related to multiethnic identity, and the majority of respondents reported that they had not had negative experiences on campus related to multiethnic identity.

Table 1: Have you ever had or witnessed a positive experience on campus related to multiethnic identity?

Yes	15	58 percent
No	11	42 percent

Table 2: Have you ever had or witnessed a negative experience on campus related to multiethnic identity?

Yes	10	38 percent
No	16	62 percent

Six respondents mentioned Mixed Student Union as being a *positive* experience, reinforcing the fact that a space for multiethnic students is necessary and beneficial for the UCLA campus.

One interesting response came from a student who does not identify as multiracial, yet still had an understanding of some of the negative experiences that many multiethnic students face:

> Talking to a few friends who are multiracial and multiethnic have had bad experiences. These friends feel like they are conflicting with both ethnic backgrounds and must choose one or the other. These feel that they cannot belong in two or more spaces and are pressured by society to lie on one part of their culture than the other.

And some feel isolated since their experiences are not relatable to those of a single ethnic group.

It is interesting to see that even those who do not identify as multiethnic can still relate to and understand the negative experiences that may come with a multiethnic identity.

Experiences with Other Ethnic/Cultural Student Groups

At UCLA, there are a large number of student groups that focus on various cultures and ethnicities. Outside of Mixed Student Union and a few others, most of these groups focus on one cultural or ethnic identity. While none of these groups would be openly discriminatory towards multiethnic students, the survey results suggest that there is still an underlying sense of unwelcome towards mixed race students in these groups. One respondent shares, "I haven't been too involved in many ethnic clubs or organizations. At the same time, I didn't feel comfortable when I tried. Nobody is intentionally or overtly exclusive, let alone mean at all; the conversations just tended towards me trying to explain why I belonged there."

Most respondents said that they avoid even trying to join such groups because of their predictions and assumptions of how they will be treated. One respondent says, "I would feel awkward joining a group that was generally for only those who are 100 percent one race, while I am mixed. Though they may not reject me outright, I would assume that they would not be quite as welcoming as if I were full." Another person explains, "I have been wary of joining the Chinese Student Association because I do not look Chinese. I've been too afraid to find out any information about them, so I honestly don't know. And as far as the Afrikan Student Union, I have not seen any mixed race kids affiliated with the club, so I haven't joined."

Other respondents explained what they have heard through word of mouth from other students who have joined these groups. One person mentioned that a family member had a negative experience with other student groups, which is why she didn't give it a chance: "I personally haven't gone to [the Japanese student group] because my sister (who is a fourth year here) told me that she felt like she didn't belong in those spaces." Another response mentions that stories from fellow sorority members deterred her from deciding to join these groups. "I feel like groups like [Afrikan Student Union] and [Nikkei Student Union] are looking for students who look and act in a way associated with their culture. I've never been to either for fear of being asked why I was there, but I have friends from my [Pan-Hellenic] sorority who are told by other members of ASU that they are too white washed." These types of sentiments reflect a bigger picture of what campus climate is like for multiethnic students.

Discussing Multiracial Topics in Ethnic Studies Courses

Often, the history of mixed race people is left out of textbooks and course readings, and therefore many of the classes revolving around race do not address the topic of mixed race. Attempts to create courses at UCLA that focus on mixed heritage and multiracial identity are challenging due to the lack of an appropriate department because they generally do not fit just one (e.g., Chicana/o studies, Asian American studies, or African American studies). However, some of the ethnic studies classes at UCLA have been known to discuss multiracial issues.

Over half of the respondents marked that they had taken a course at UCLA that addressed issues of race and ethnicity, however they also responded that many of the courses, with a few exceptions, either breezed over multiracial identity and history or ignored it completely. One student who had taken quite a few of these courses noted, "The professors for these courses were all multiethnic individuals. In a standard course with a different professor, I don't know if they'd bother to do more than skim over multiethnic class materials."

Changing Perspectives about Mixed Identity

By learning about what causes students' perspectives about mixed identity to change, we can gain a better understanding of "what works" and how to move forward. In this survey, four respondents mentioned Mixed Student Union as helping them to change their perspectives. Some respondents recalled how Mixed Student Union allowed them to learn more about multiethnic studies: "I joined Mixed Student Union and learned more about how other mixed people viewed themselves, and what academic literature exists on the mixed experience," "Being a part of Mixed Student Union has allowed me to learn about not only my own identity, but the history of multiethnic people and how it affects our everyday lives. In some ways I feel more comfortable with my identity now, but I'm also more conscious of the ways my multiethnic identity makes me an outcast." Others talked about how the student group allowed them to understand other student's experiences and learn more about their own: "MSU has allowed me to see other mixed people's perspectives on their own identities which has helped me reinforce my own ideas on my personal identity," "Joining MSU, I have become a lot more aware of the different types of multiethnic identities there are and I realized that everyone has had a different experience. I also became a lot more aware of how we are NOT represented and how this is something that needs to be more brought up."

One person mentioned the classroom as a reason for changing their perspective: "I learned about a much wider range of multiethnic people and their experiences. Previously, I had only talked to a few half Asian people around my age." Many respondents explained that they are much more aware of the existence of a growing multiethnic population. "It was just something that was there before and now I'm realizing more people that are. They don't necessarily fit on one side or the other but they prefer to choose and be part of a group." One respondent who did not identify as being multiracial personally felt that their perspectives changed about what his Hapa friends were going through:

> It changed, because I got to understand some personal and structural issues of being multiethnic. I wouldn't say I was living in a color-blind society, but as an optimist, I really did think that multiethnic people were welcomed, because I welcome anyone in any race/ background. However, having some Hapa friends made me realize that their struggles are different from my own. Instead of just oppression and colonialism they face, they also need to make drastic changes of their identity to feel fit onto this campus, when it should not be a case. Even the Census segregates multiethnic people, since there is not a bubble for them to circle.

Lastly, a few respondents talked about how being at UCLA in general helped change their perspectives on multiethnic identity and where they fall in a racial/social hierarchy: "I think previous to coming to UCLA it wasn't something I thought about often or really noticed. I have a few friends back home that come from multiethnic backgrounds but I don't think it was talked about as much as it is now. It's something I talk about now and want to understand better." Another shared, "I am much more aware of my ethnicities. I went to school with the same people all my life, so they knew that I was Black and Chinese. At UCLA no one really knew, so I started getting all these questions about it. Now I realize just how important multiethnic identity is to people who are not multiethnic."

The Representation of Diversity on Campus

In the final question of the survey, students were asked if they felt diversity was well represented on the UCLA campus in general (i.e., not just in relation to multiethnicity). About half responded, "no," and a third "yes," with four checking "I don't know." When asked to comment on their choice, the responses varied, but many fell along common lines. Many cited the statistics released by the UCLA admissions office, which are often used as a source of pride by the school, saying that they are misleading. Similarly, others responded that while they can physically see some diversity on campus, the representation of certain groups is undoubtedly unequal. Others highlighted the lack of crossover between cultural groups, stating that it creates a divided campus. Of the responses from those who checked "yes," one in particular stood out:

> [There is a] ridiculous variety of backgrounds at UCLA and seems like almost all minorities are over represented. If you change or increase the acceptances to "increase diversity" you'll just be lowering UCLA's prestige and devaluing our degrees. This "diversity crisis" is unfounded and if anything is just going to end up hurting the school.

While this response is in itself a minority opinion in the context of the survey responses, this does not make its message less significant. Such opinions are prime examples of misinformation regarding university admissions, especially concerning affirmative action. It also serves as reinforcement of the purpose of this survey. Clearly, misinformation or a lack of education on what diversity can really mean on such a large campus still exists. Responses such as these only make changes even more clearly needed.

Recommendations for Moving Forward

It is clear that these limited survey responses cannot adequately reflect the feelings of the UCLA campus as a whole, which is why our primary recommendation for the future is expanding the survey base. With more responses, the campus climate for multiracial, multiethnic, and multicultural students could be better assessed. This would allow for more concrete interpretation of the results, which could lead to more applicable improvements. The survey need not necessarily be stand-alone; instead, it could be incorporated into the annual campus climate survey. In this way, UCLA could not only formally acknowledge the presence and influence of multiracial students on the campus, but also begin to collect data on the demographic. Similarly, addressing the presence of mixed race students on campus would help to foster a diverse and educated environment for students who may not themselves identify as mixed.

After recognition, there are further changes that we would like to see be made. One of these is the establishment of a multiethnic studies center. This would give a home to the multiethnic studies courses that already exist at UCLA, and the faculty who focus on multiethnic topics. The center could also offer a multiethnic studies minor to further encourage students to take these courses. Few to none of the ethnic studies courses offered discuss multiracial identity, history, or challenges. And, even when such courses are offered, they are placed within another ethnic department, making it very difficult for students to find the classes to enroll in. For example, this paper is a product of a fiat lux course titled "Being Mixed Race at UCLA," and is considered a course in Chicana and Chicano studies. At the beginning of the quarter, students were asked how they found out about the class, and all nineteen replied that they had heard from word of mouth or that they had stumbled upon the class in the course catalog. Not only would a center allow for easier access by students to classes revolving around issues of multiethnicity, but also the advancement of mixed race studies, inclusive discourse, and the solidification of multiracial people as a unique ethnic group on campus and in academia.

Similarly, we would like to have greater formal recognition by the UCLA administration in varying areas of the UCLA experience. Currently, UCLA does not use inclusive language to acknowledge the multiethnic student and faculty population. One of the biggest issues we have found is our lack of representation in the UCLA Undergraduate Admissions Statistics. In the section on student ethnicity, there is no category for multiracial students, which begs the question: where do they place mixed students? If a student marks, for example, African American *and* Asian, is that student part of the "African American/Black" percentage, or the "Asian/Pacific Islander" percentage? Not only is this representation important for multiethnic students, but it would also serve as a more honest indicator of UCLA's diversity. If mixed race students are simply placed in whatever category is a smaller minority, those statistics do not truly represent the ethnicities on our campus. Multiracial people are the fastest growing ethnic demographic in America, and it is time we are recognized as a legitimate and influential group on this campus.

Part II: Theoretical Reflections on Mixed Race

Unconscious Desire in Microaggressions: Self-Reflections from a Perpetrator-Recipient in a Mixed Race Context

Lisa Yamasaki

This paper combines a theoretical discussion and personal reflection to depict my interpretation of my own personal experience as a mixed race individual. I initially define my notion of mixed race subjectivity as a state of being that comprises two or more different histories and narratives, yielding liberated yet conflicted feelings. In my experience, my particular racial blend blurs the distinctions others can make about my racial makeup. While many see me as distinctively "not white," many also are not able to accurately racially identify me; perplexed by this ambiguity, most conclude in their initial impressions of me that race is not a factor in my life. I am predominately Latina mixed with Asian descent, yet most people attribute other ethnicities to me; this has presented different ways for me to identify. Such ambiguity was a product of being a recipient of microaggressions and a motivating factor for wrongly perpetuating microaggressions.

I first define microaggressions and explain a particular example where the perpetrator-recipient is mixed race, thus showing my internalized racism from years of being a victim of racial microaggressions. By investigating racial identity in critical race theory and post-structuralist theories and mixed race, I then describe the way that each perspective contributes to deconstructing microaggressions. Next, using a French post-structuralist conceptualization of desire, I depict the underlying layers of desire within one type of racial microaggression, thus unveiling unconscious factors that may contradict motives from the conscious level in the transaction of a microaggression.

Microaggressions in a Mixed Race Context

For the purpose of this paper, I limit my discussion to the possibility of a tendency of a mixed race person to occupy the position of perpetrator-recipient due to experiences of exclusion from any given monoracially-constructed group. Unlike many forms of microaggressions that are overtly racist, the covert examples of microaggressions present a danger in luring the uncritical recipient, who in turn may internalize the racism and become a perpetrator. Other forms of microaggressions reveal obvious racist gestures towards students of color in interpersonal spaces, racist jokes, rejection from academic spaces, and cultural starvation, or institutional practices that negate the lived experiences of people of color (Yosso, Smith, Ceja, and Solórzano 2009; Solórzano 2001). Daniel Solórzano (1998) posits a few examples that people of color with a certain amount of privilege—intellectual capital, social and cultural capital, and a light phenotype—witness as racially charged statements often concealed in the form of a "compliment."

Marc Johnston and Kevin Nadal (2010) define monoracial as "the social system of psychological inequality where individuals who do not fit monoracial categories may be oppressed on systematic and interpersonal levels because of underlying assumptions and beliefs in singular, discrete racial categories" (Johnston and Nadal 2010, 125). Monoracism is a form of racism that forms the foundation for the microaggressions targeted at mixed race people when they feel excluded from a racial community and unable to express their identities as multiracial people. Many of these individuals feel the need to identify with one race due to pressure from social environments. Johnston and Nadal (2010) reveal that some studies show stress caused in interpersonal interactions as seen when racial jokes are made in the presence of multiracial people due to being perceived as not belonging to a particular racial category. In fact, Johnston and Nadal (2010) list five forms of microaggressions towards multiracial people: feelings of exclusion, objectification, mistaken identity or assumption of monoracial identity, denial of multiracial identity, and perceived as psychologically abnormal (Johnston and Nadal, 2010). With the different criteria suggesting that perpetrators can be people of color, microaggressions can validate offense taken when one is assumed to belong solely to one racial group.

Yet there is danger if mixed race individuals internalize perceived honorary status or preferential treatment as indications of being superior to their monoracial minority peers. Arising from feelings of superiority is the possibility of a person of mixed racial identity to further enact microaggressions upon other people of color. Referring to perpetrators of microaggressions as perpetrator-recipient, I consider that internalized racism within a perpetrator-recipient originates from collective instances of being recipients of racial microaggressions. Initially, the perpetrators of color are victims of microaggressions that involve a white perpetrator. Since my racial heritage is predominantly Latina, I specify my discussion of microaggressions to only refer to statements such as "I had no idea you were Latina," or "You are not like a Latina," which can be classified as a microaggression of mistaken identity or the assumption of monoracial identity. I, as a mixed race Latina recipient, internalized the comment to suggest that I had some power, albeit a delusion, similar to the white perpetrator, thus making it justifiable to assert superiority over my monoracial peers. Thus, one goal is to identify the various layers of microaggressions especially for multiracial individuals, who could potentially feel the impulse to become perpetrator-recipients, whether consciously or unconsciously.

Critical Race Theory and Latino Racial Identity

A critical race theoretical framework in education has five central themes: (1) a strong focus on race, racism, and other manifestations of subordination, (2) a challenge to dominant ideology, or a revolt against theoretical frameworks and practices that support meritocracy, color-blindness, and race neutrality, (3) an enactment of social justice by eradicating racism in its theoretical premise or application of theory, (4) an emphasis on experiential knowledge either in methodology or incorporation in theory, and (5) an incorporation of many disciplines or interdisciplinary perspectives, or a combination of different critical and social theories (Solórzano 1997; Delgado Bernal 2002; Yosso and Solórzano 2005; Solórzano and Yosso 2001). LatCrit Theory is a sub-division in Critical Race Theory, which focuses specifically on the Latina/o community. Lindsey Perez Huber (2009) defines LatCrit as a theoretical framework that examines the varied experiences of Latina/os as reflected in differences in phenotype, immigration status, ethnicity, language, culture and identity. One object of study for LatCrit scholars is the role that Latina/os share with other minorities in raising awareness of their marginalization despite that they may have whiteness as part of their racial identities.

Enid Trucios-Haynes (2001) demands that Latina/os define their racial identity and form coalitions with other communities of color to stop white supremacy and its concomitant racial hierarchical social practices. For instance, she indicates that their indeterminate status in a Black-white racial paradigm causes a splintering of communities of color, especially amongst Latina/os. While some Latina/os experience acceptance from the mainstream by exhibiting signs of whiteness, others are further differentiated and discriminated. The dynamic Latina/o racial identity is comprised of different cultures and ethnicities and entails the possibilities of diverse experiences that Latina/os experience in a racialized society. Richard Delgado (2004) further exemplifies this point in his book review essay, "Locating Latinos in the Field of Civil Rights," which describes George Yancey's book, *Who is White?* and Yancey's perspective on the assimilation process in Latina/os and their acceptance into the white spaces. While Delgado is critical of Yancey's claim of Latina/os and Asians as the "new whites," his analysis presents evidence that these minorities benefit from learning to navigate white culture as they move into white neighborhoods and send their children to predominantly white schools. The binary causes Asian and Latina/o minorities to choose a white or Black position, thus inferring the tendency for many to choose the white paradigm (Delgado 2004). Within this literature, the mixed racial status of different Latina/os is acknowledged, yet these individuals cannot express their sense of belonging to different racial groups. By affirming a monoracial status, they only have the option of affirming a Latina/o racial identity—Black position—or a racially benign position—the approximation to the white option.

Using a CRT/LatCrit lens, the overtly racist implication is that the multiracially-identifying individual offends his or her monoracially-identifying Latina/o peers by upholding a multiracial identity option;

however the offense suggests that the multiracial individual should repress a multiracial identity, and thereby deny one's heritage in order to be "Latina/o"--there is little space to be "both/and" as evidenced in Renn (2004) and other scholarly work on multiracial identity. In other words, to not simply identity as Latina suggests that I intend to express my own self-hate, when actually, I am expressing my pride in being part Latina. In my experience, even my physical manifestation of multiracial identity seemed to elicit scorn or incredulous looks from some monoracially-constructed groups. On the contrary, some monoracially-constructed groups commented on my fortunate ability to look distinct, even suggesting that my difference in appearance made me "lovely." In these instances, these people did not consider my similarities to them, such as my dark hair, dark eyes, and skin tone, thus compelling me to perceive myself as "different due to being Latina and Asian." Yet, I could not openly affirm this identity, thus making me only perceive microaggressions in terms of how well I belonged to the Latina/o or Asian group, given that I did not feel that I belonged exclusively to any one group. Thus the CRT/LatCrit framework explains my experiences as an expression of my own self-hate by agreeing with the white perpetrator that I was indeed atypical for a Latina or an Asian; however, this interpretation is inaccurate and incomplete; a further understanding can be had through post-structural and mixed race identity theories.

Post-structuralist Theory and Mixed Race

One side effect of repressing one's mixed race status is that it could lead to intellectualizing characteristics in identity by referring to them as signifiers and contradictions inherent in upholding any particular identity. In his essay, "Mimicry and Man," Homi Bhaba (1994) describes mimicry as a discourse produced by interdiction, or the process in a discourse in which the person enacts a difference that negates his/her identity. It is a discourse between two different fields or signifiers in which one signifier must be concealed while the other is acknowledged and affirmed. This concept describes a split subject, or the idea that one's image registers metonymic presence of two or more contrasting histories, narratives, and races. Bhaba's essay articulates a subjectivity of contradictory discourses; one that affirms the colonial power and another, which disavows it making the colonized troubled. In the context of mixed racial identity, I perceive that different discourses traverse through mixed race individuals. A mixed race person's identity is constructed from interactions in different environments, each comprising one layer of identity. This concept is borrowed from Jacques Lacan's notion of mimicry, which he defines as an act of camouflaging, not that one should conceal with one's environment, rather the central issue is that an act of mimicry entails the idea that something within someone requires to be concealed (Lacan 1998). With prevalent unconscious racism often brought about by repression of a mixed race status, it is easy to see how one's environment requires racially mixed individuals to adopt a notion of racial ambiguity, particularly if they do not internally identify with a singular monoracial category that is congruent with their physical appearance.

To be racially ambiguous is to be undefined, thus one can have entry into different racial circles and yet feel isolated. To uphold a racially ambiguous identity is synonymous to the phenomenon of passing for white. In the short story, *Passing*, in which two African American women share two separate perspectives on passing, Larsen defines passing as a "breaking away from all that was familiar and friendly to take one's chance in another environment, not entirely strange, perhaps, but certainly not entirely friendly. What, for example, one did about background, how one accounted for oneself" (2001, 186-187). While one woman, Clare Kendry, completely fabricated her background, the other female character, Irene, functions as her foil, a witness to the result of Clare's reintroduction into her social circles.

Clare's ability to partake in both worlds while being stranger to both aptly describes my experience of being mixed race, in which I have always felt akin to a fragment of both my Latina and Asian identities, yet a stranger to both social circles. Similar to racial passing as portrayed in Larsen's story, my early grappling with adopting a monoracial identity arose from my interactions with my white peers through a series of discourses where I presented a narrative of racial minority that simultaneously lessened the threat yet affirmed dominant views of other minorities. Like the colonized subject in Homi Bhaba's essay, I found myself in a contradiction—I used to mimic white gestures only to uncover that I was always perceived as distinct, despite transient moments of racial invisibility. By responding to one's own repression of a mixed race status by identifying as racially ambiguous, it brings up the notion that there are many environments that mixed race people camouflage whether or not they actively seek it. Yet, the underlying issue in such repression is that it develops due to the mindset that all individuals—monoracial and mixed race individuals—lack a complete identity, since a claim for wholeness is replete with contradiction. Thus, while post-structuralist theory provided me intellectual stimulus and affirmation of an edgy identity as a split subject, it could not help me deal with the damage in the presumption that monoracial identities were easier to process on a structural level.

Literature on Mixed Racial Identity

The literature on mixed race identity substantiated my different experiences of self-identifying as belonging to two races, upholding a multiracial label, or even upholding a postmodernist belief in split subjectivity. While a historical trajectory of the mixed race identity formation is beneficial for any kind of discussion on the matter, I only discuss scholars pertinent to this paper. Kristen Renn (2000) discovered a person's sense of private and public space impacted his or her ability to assert a multiracial identity. Even though some of the students she interviewed expressed a need to assert their racial identities and sought out different groups, some felt a paradoxical pushback due to the groups' need to force them to uphold a monoracial identity. Some students expressed a need to legitimate certain racial identities, especially when they were judged for not having stereotypical physical traits from one of their racial and ethnic backgrounds (Renn 2000).

Expanding further on the "ecological model," by using Uri Bronfenbrenner's model, Kristen Renn (2003) articulates five different ways that multiracial students identify: upholding and merging multiple perspectives, shifting between different racial identities, upholding a multiracial identity, upholding a monoracial identity, and deconstructing race as a discursive category. By seeking to provide a model for mixed race individuals that allows for a plurality of experiences, Renn describes that these individuals self-identify according to the social environments in which they participate. Renn's work builds on earlier studies of mixed racial identities, including the works of scholars who describe fluidity in racial identity that encompasses both a relational and experiential process (Gatson 2003) and others who show that a multiracial identity encompasses participation with different monoracial groups, even those groups that wish to claim mixed race individuals due to a resemblance in appearance (Williams 1996). In addition to Renn (2000, 2003), Rockquemore, Brunsma, and Delgado (2009) articulate that multiracial individuals exhibit different ways of identifying racially due to fluctuations in social context (Renn 2000, 2003; Rockquemore, Brunsma, and Delgado 2009). Since mixed racial identity focuses predominantly on participation in different monoracial groups, the way of conceptualizing microaggressions for mixed race individuals takes a different structure. When examining the experiences of other mixed raced individuals, I am not as compelled to repress my mixed racial identity as I did in my earlier years, thus allowing me to recognize the racism others have revealed through their comments on my racial identity. By presuming I am not Latina or in some cases, presuming that I use my differences to mask a monoracial Latina identity, others have revealed their monoracism. In pontificating a particular psychoanalytical structure to microaggressions, I unveil traces of desire that the perpetrator reveals to the victim on an unconscious level, while using the mask of insults to do so.

Lacan's Structure on Desire

In Jacques Lacan's early psychoanalytic theory, he describes a model of subjectivity in which human beings situate themselves according to the desire of the other. As a subject of desire, the subject wants the desire of the other, as opposed to the desire for the other. Yet, there is no determinate number of ways that a subject constitutes himself/herself through the other. The desire of the other is described in speech in the form of a signifier leading to other signifiers, or verbal or image of something, and these signifiers have an indefinite number of forms of desire—intellectual desire, sexual desire, desire for world peace, and so on (Desire Seminar 1959). In his Desire Seminar, Lacan depicts three stages of desire. The first stage consists of the mirror-stage or identification through images and primary narcissism. The Mirror Stage consists of a young infant's corporeal identification with one's spectral image. The child establishes himself/herself as a subject through identifying with a certain image. The child perceives that s/he is independent of his/her caretaker's nurture, since the spectral image reflects the child apart from his/her parents. Yet, there is a twist to this independence. In so far as the child formulates an ideal ego—an ideal image of oneself—s/he also misrecognizes his/her independence from others as the initial way to conceptualize the self. It is this misrecognition that forms a bias in all social relations (Lacan and Ecrit 1949). Thus, this primary stage explains for racial segregation at a young age, in which children might feel a tendency to identify with others based on their physical "mirrored" image to another person of a similar race. Similar to the illusion of the virtual image that most people take as the real view, identification with others solely based on racial mirrored appearance is a misrecognition of oneself [1].

The secondary stage of desire constitutes a secondary level of narcissism, leading to identification with finding oneself in another person since one situates his/her position according to the conditions of one's own particular environment. Lacan gives the term libidinal being, a being whose position is based on his relations with others. He alludes to the ego-ideal, the critical agency that helps the subject establish an ideal. This differs from the ideal ego, since the ego-ideal is a stricter guide navigating the subject's actions in social relations using speech. Narcissism comes into play because the subject longs for something s/he has lost, and the establishment of the ego-ideal develops through a searching within oneself to find something similar to oneself exterior to oneself in social contexts (Lacan 1991).

The third stage of desire centers on the gap in one's realization that one's desire and subjectivity relates to the desire of the other. Much of this realization arises in the contradictions and paradoxes in one's speech. In so far as Lacan emphasizes the signifier as the key to unravel the mysteries of one's desire, the subject's transformation into a structure of signifiers

---

[1] In his seminar, *Freud's Papers on Technique*, he addresses the level of narcissism in social relations due to the ego formation during the initial identification of self. He presents an optical schema in which a person at a certain angle is able to perceive a virtual image of an inverted bouquet of flowers despite the fact that the vase is inverted under a bouquet of flowers. With the use of a concave mirror, this trick shows that a virtual image replaces that of a real image, and Lacan uses this apparatus to illustrate the way in which subjects self-identify and form the illusion that the corporeal image shelters our ego as the vase does with the flowers (Lacan 1991).

suggests a structural composition of the subject's relationship to desire (Lacan 1959). It is this stage that is relevant to uncovering the ways in which recipients of microaggressions can interpret them as simultaneous forms of highly charged racism and a threat that perpetrators feel but cannot express in a more honest and genuine fashion.

Lacan's three stages of desire as subjectivity provide the background to better understand one possible way that a mixed race person succumbs to racial invisibility due to wrongful notions of desire. When I was younger, I was not as consciously aware of the effects that microaggressions had on me, thus I did not critically question their function. Therefore, I am looking retrospectively on times where microaggressions occurred. I do not discuss one particular occasion, rather the way that many instances of microaggressions force me to consider their collective impact. For me, I describe a white perpetrator's identification with my desire for white privilege—or racial invisibility, honorary minority status—can function in various degrees of primary and secondary narcissism, given my prolonged exposure to colorblind ideas and meritocracy.

It is possible that the perpetrator identified with me due to my racial ambiguity in my appearance. Furthermore, the similarities in our social and intellectual interests demonstrate the process of identification through conversation, the types Homi Bhaba refers to when talking about interdiction. Yet my discussion on microaggressions sheds some light as to how desire functions in interdiction. Bhaba states: "[C]olonial mimicry is the desire for a reformed recognizable Other, *as a subject of a difference that is almost the same, but not quite.* Which is to say, that the discourse of mimicry is constructed around an *ambivalence*; in order to be effective mimicry must continually produce its slippage, its excess, its difference" (1994, 122).

Thus, in my situation, when the perpetrator made the aforementioned comments, s/he considered it a compliment, and I perceived it as such given the nature of identification, or the qualities praised and affirmed in the dominant culture. In my case, I also situated my subjectivity on the white perpetrator's desire, which could stand for more uncritical assumptions about race. The microaggressions functioned as compliments—affirmations of whiteness—yet also paradoxically also a difference that allows for the perpetrator to safely identify with parts of me while noting my difference. Within an unconscious level, desire unleashes itself through different words, despite also conveying a plurality in meaning.

Lacan's third stage of desire as the realization of the gap in one's words clarifies the way the microaggressions reveal the perpetrator's sense of threat by identifying with me. The gap in one's realization of an internal split in one's identity manifests itself in the form of crudely formulated statements (Lacan 1959). The perpetrator and I both perceive the microaggressions represent an indication of my difference from others belonging to my race or ethnicity. As a signifier, the microaggression represents a split in the perpetrator's subjectivity, one affirmed in the recipient's existence as a person who negates the perpetrator's understanding of the norm. An understanding of the third stage of subjectivity as desire necessitates a brief explanation of Lacan's notion of shifting signifier or the signifier-to-signifier relationship in speech.

In a traditional psychoanalytic setting, the subject loses his/her will and succumbs to the desire of the analyst, thus alluding to Lacan's death of the subject through discourse. This notion of death is not a literal death of the subject, but one in discourse in which the subject disappears from his/her own discourse (Lacan 1953). Language also constitutes bodily symptoms, as an expression of one's position with regards to desire. Other forms of language include childhood memories, one's particular vocabulary and form of self-expression, historical sociocultural traditions, and traces of negation in one's speech such as a slip of a tongue or "unintentional" use of words (Lacan 1953, 2006). These define other articulations in addition—and sometimes in contradiction to—one's speech. While speech may suffer from actually signifying an object in-itself, the meandering in meaning indicates a plurality in interpretation. As the subject articulates himself/herself through speech, s/he experiences a split between the enunciated words and the process of enunciating as well as phenomenon called *aphransis*—the disappearance of the subject due to being reduced to a signifier (Lacan 1999). To clarify, the split in the enunciated and the enunciating refers to the difference between the process of speaking and the words themselves. Thus, the unconscious stores the subject's desire and reveals it through contradictory gaps in the subject's speech. By locating it through examination of signifiers, or different words and images, one can find traces of the unconscious, hence fragments of the subject's subjectivity.

It is mapped out clearly when taking Lacan's description of a simple sentence showing the subjective complement. In his unpublished seminar, *Identification*, Lacan (1962) expounds on the difference between a signifier and a sign. While a sign represents something for someone else, the signifier leads to a difference between two objects or humans compared to each other in the sentence (e.g., "A is A"). Usually in language conventions, the subject and the subject complement are closely related, yet Lacan is questioning it in his assertions. He is indicating that the properties of the first A do not match those of the second A precisely due to function of the signifier as leading to differences between the two A's (Lacan 1962). Also, Lacan's notion of the shifting signifier (i.e. the idea in which the sound or image of an object does not necessarily only refer to its concept but to another signifier) is relevant in this discussion. His overturning of the signifier to signified relationship to a signifier-to-signifier relationship can explain the manner by which statements are not conclusive to the speaker's intent, thus showing the underlying meanings in an utterance. The structure of desire and shifting signifier show a different inner structure to microaggressions.

The Role of Desire in Microaggressions

Before I show the layers of desire, I offer one interpretation of microaggressions using the framework of signifiers and the subject's relationship to the desire of the other. In addition, I also show the way by which identification occurs through contradiction—finding similarities through difference. The microaggressions represent my perpetrator's sense of threat when encountering me. When s/he states that I am not like the others in my race, one can perceive a double negation of the second part of the sentence. Taking the words literally, "You are not like them," the pronoun "you" represents me, and "not like them" stands for the subjective complement. A literal interpretation of Lacan's discussion of the signifier shows a double negation of the subjective complement. Given that Lacan asserts A is not A, one can read the microaggression as "You are not different from them," having the "A is not A" or "A is A" function. In negating herself while asserting the "complement," the perpetrator is actually stating that I am similar to one group comprising my racial background, but the perpetrator herself cannot determine my racial makeup, thus allowing her to identify with me due to a lack of specific racial identifiers. If the perpetrator does not recognize racial multidimensionality, this identification shows that the perpetrator feels confused as to identify with a person of color. Therefore, the microaggression represents the perpetrator's threat from the recipient causing a rupture in her understanding of her own subjectivity. Her desire has led her to a person she did not foresee.

When I recall the numerous times that I received such remarks, I realize that I unconsciously had recognized the threat embedded within them, but I refused to acknowledge the deeper implications. Instead, I consciously desired to continue existing in the liminal space of racial ambiguity—passing, or my disingenuous honorary white status causing an internalization of my perpetrator's threat. I embraced my different facets of my racial identity, yet I still claimed difference in the face of my Latina/o peers. Resuming to my experience as the perpetrator-recipient, the inverse of my interactions with my white peers occurred during my interactions with monoracial Latina/os. After internalizing the racism inherent in the initial verbal assault ("You are not like them"), I repressed the primary and secondary identification with a potential recipient, another Latina. I felt the threat of my difference was slowly fading and more of our similarities appeared in our interactions—an internal monologue might be "I am like them." In this situation, the desire structure between the new recipient of the microaggression, another Latina, and me varies depending on my desire. I focused more on highlighting the differences rather than using our similarities to broach the subject of our differences.

Upon further reflection, however, I perceive another explanation for partial desire for whiteness and acknowledgement from monoracial groups. During my adolescence and earlier adulthood years, I opted to remain entrenched in my liminal state, desiring to present my racial mix as a form of invisibility, creating new signifiers without addressing that my premise was founded on oppressive stereotypes. Yet, after considering that I myself furthered monoracism by closing myself off to the monoracial Latina/o groups, I did not seek the opportunity to further address my previous forms of repression. I was repressed due to my lack of power evident in my white peers but also in my inability to participate in monoracial groups; thus I upheld my difference only to further separate myself. While I consciously admitted my desire for whiteness, or rather, the ability to walk through social circles without making racial identity an issue—as might be the case with different monoracial and mixed race individuals—I never questioned the fact that such an unconscious desire blocked me from my own process of unhinging my repressed pain of exclusion from many groups.

The aforementioned example of microaggression does exemplify the desire of the other through different modes of identification such as the use of physical appearance (first stage of desire), recognition through social interaction (second stage of desire), and the realization that the other completes us through our own split subjectivity (third stage of desire). Yet, it is possible that the microaggression, rather than only depicting unconscious monoracism, also expresses an unconscious desire to be similar to those whose perceived differences only serve as limitations in one's own identity formation. In his article, "The Id, the Ego, and Equal Protection: Reckoning with Unconscious Racism," Charles Lawrence III (1987) describes verbal microaggressions as slips of the mind that are not critically examined on a regular basis from a large group of people, thus they become codified as stereotypes in mainstream culture. I further this idea in the example of monoracist microaggressions, where the perpetrators can be other monoracial minorities, multiracial minorities, or whites who assume that one has a monoracial identity. Even in the case of monoracist microaggressions, where the insult relates to an assumption of a monoracial identity upon a mixed race individual, the perceived differences in physical appearance or gestures that shift from the white perpetrator and monoracial perpetrator of color suggest unconscious fear of having limitations of one's own complete subjectivity. Furthermore, the incompletion of one's subjectivity suggests that it requires identification with others to give some notion of completion. Consequently, it is erroneous to only perceive microaggressions as exclusively encompassing racist thinking rather than simultaneously eliciting a desire to know the other to complete the self. The slips of the mind function as crude explorations from one's knowledge of another's racial identity to the unknown, a term I use to denote the limitations of one's own knowledge of a person's mixed racial identity. In return, it is also crucial for the mixed race perpetrator-recipient to not internalize such slips of the mind when associating with other monoracial minorities and critically examine his or her deeper motives for inflicting cruel assumptions from monoracial individuals. Therefore, while I am not minimizing the pain associated with receiving microaggressions, I am asserting that they could also reveal masked desire within perpetrators, which exposes them to vulnerability when making their comments.

Conclusion

As indicated in the mixed race literature, one's racial identity process is highly dependent on the person's social environment. Hurtado, Alvarado, and Guillermo-Wann (2015) examine racial identity salience through a conceptual model, the Multicontextual Model for Diverse Learning Environments, which incorporates educational processes and practices in classrooms and co-curricular spaces. If activities are centered on building awareness of racial diversity and difference, then the students have stronger racial identities. Part of the activities on building awareness on racial diversity is to deconstruct microaggressions for the purpose of unveiling both the victim's understanding of them, the perpetrator's motive for making the comments, any internalization process that perpetrator-recipients harbor, and the unconscious aspects of these comments.

By having mixed race individuals speak about their experiences, it would contribute to the goals of critical race theory literature, mixed race literature, and educational goals for diverse learning environments. After reading various accounts on mixed race experiences, I realize that I am not alone in my experiences, yet many of the narratives only discuss being victims of monoracial microaggressions. By also being held accountable as a perpetrator, I demonstrate an issue that arose with my experiences, thus I infer that unless more open conversations about race are broached there is more of a possibility of mixed race individuals to hold the contradictory position of perpetrator-recipient and their conflicting unconscious desires internalized from monoracial white perpetrators. My analysis of the desire structure of the perpetrator-recipient of microaggressions sheds light on the inner conflicts possible within some Latina/os whose mixed racial identity allows for racial invisibility. In doing so, I want to diversify narratives for any racial experience; being mixed race is just a part of being part of the racial groups that comprise a mixed raced individual's identity.

Bibliography

Bhabha, Homi K. *The Location of Culture*. London & New York: Routledge, 1994.

Delgado-Bernal, Dolores. "Critical Race Theory, Latino Critical Theory, and Critical Raced- Gendered Epistemologies: Recognizing Students of Color as Holders and Creators of Knowledge." *Qualitative Inquiry* 8, no. 1, (2002): 105-126.

Delgado, Richard. "Locating Latinos in the Field of Civil Rights: Assessing the Neoliberal Case for Racial Exclusion: Who is White? Latinos, Asians, and the New Black/Nonblack divide." *Texas Law Review* 83, no. 2 (December 2004): 489-524.

Erickson, Erik. *Identity: Youth and Crisis*. New York: W. W. Norton Company. 1968.

Gatson, Sarah. "On Being Amorphous: Autoethnography, Genealogy, and a Multiracial Identity." *Qualitative Inquiry* 9, no. 1(February 2003): 20-38.

Hurtado, S., Adriana R. Alvarado, and Chelsea Guillermo-Wann. "Thinking About Race: The Salience of Racial Identity at Two-and Four-Year Colleges and the Climate for Diversity." *Journal of Higher Education* 86, no. 1(2015): 127-155.

Johnston, M., and Kevin L. Nadal. "Multiracial Microaggressions: Exposing Monoracism in Everyday Life and Clinical Practice." In *Microaggressions and Marginality: Manifestation, Dynamics, and Impacts,* edited by Derald Wing Sue, 123-144. New York: Wiley & Sons, 2010.

Lacan, Jacques. "The Function and Field of Speech and Language in Psychoanalysis." In *Écrits: The First Complete Edition in English*. Translated by Bruce Fink. New York: W.W. Norton, 2007.

Lacan, Jacques. *The Seminar of Jacques Lacan: The Four Fundamental Concepts of Psychoanalysis*. Edited by Jacques-Alain Miller. Translated by Alan Sheridan. New York: W. W. Norton & Company, 1978.

Lacan, Jacques. *The Ethics of Psychoanalysis: The Seminar of Jacques Lacan. 1959-1960*. Edited by Jacques-Alain Miller. Translated by Dennis Porter. London: Routledge, 1992.

Lacan, Jacques. *Freuds Papers on Technique, 1953-1954.* Edited by Jacques-Alain Miller. Translated by John Forrester. New York: W.W. Norton, 1993.

Lacan, Jacques. *Identification.* Translated by Cormac Gallagher. 1962. http://www.lacaninireland.com/web/wp-content/uploads/2010/06/Seminar-IX-Amended-Iby-MCL-7.NOV_.20111.pdf

Lacan, J. (1959). *Desire and Its Interpretation.* Translated by Cormac Gallagher. 1959. http://www.lacaninireland.com/web/wp-content/uploads/2010/06/Book-06-Desire-and-its-interpretation.pdf

Larsen, Nella. "Passing" In *The Complete Fiction of Nella Larsen.* Edited by C. R. Larson. New York: Archor Books, 2001.

Lawrence III, Charles. "The Id, the Ego, and Equal Protection: Reckoning with Unconscious Racism." *Stanford Law Review* 39, no. 2 (1987): 317-388.

Perez Huber, Lindsay. "Disrupting Apartheid of Knowledge: Testimonio as Methodology in Latina/o Critical Race Research in Education." *International Journal of Qualitative Studies in Education* 22, no. 6 (November 2009): 639-654.

Poston, Walker C. "The Biracial Identity Development Model: A Needed Addition." *Journal of Counseling and Development,* 69, no. 2 (November 1990): 152-155.

Renn, Kristen A. "Understanding the Identities of Mixed-Race College Students Through a Developmental Ecology Lens." *Journal of College Student Development* 44, no. 3 (May 2003): 383-403.

Renn, Kristen A. "Patterns of Situational Identity Among Biracial and Multiracial College Students." *The Review of Higher Education* 23, no. 4 (Summer 2000): 399-420.

Rockquemore, K., David Brunsma, and Daniel J. Delgado. "Racing to Theory or Retheorizing Race? Understanding the Struggle to Build a Multiracial Identity Theory." *Journal of Social Issues* 65, no. 1 (January 2009): 13-34.

Solórzano, Daniel G. "Critical Race Theory, Race and Gender Microaggressions, and the Experience of Chicana and Chicano Scholars." *Qualitative Studies in Education* 11, no. 1 (January 1998): 121-136.

Solórzano, Daniel G. "Images and Words that Wound: Critical Race Theory, Racial Stereotyping, and Teacher Education." *Teacher Education Quarterly* 24, no. 3 (Summer 1997): 5-19.

Solórzano, D.G. & Tara J. Yosso. "Critical Race and LatCrit Theory and Method: Counter-storytelling Chicana and Chicano Graduate School Experiences." *Qualitative Studies in Education* 14, no. 4 (July 2001): 471-495.

Trucios-Haynes, Enid. "Why 'Race Matters': LatCrit Theory and Latina/o Racial Identity." *La Raza Law Journal* 12, no. 1 (2000): 1-42.

Yosso, T., William A. Smith, Miguel Ceja, and Daniel G. Solórzano. "Critical Race Theory, Racial Microaggressions, and Campus Racial Climate for Latina/o Undergraduates." *Harvard Educational Review* 79, no. 4, (December 2009): 659-960.

Yosso, T. & Daniel G. Solórzano. "Conceptualizing a Critical Race Theory in Sociology." In *The Blackwell Companion to Social Inequalities*, edited by Mary Romero and Eric Margolis, 117-146. Hoboken, NJ: Wiley-Blackwell Publishing, 2005.

Williams, Teresa K. "Race as Process: Reassessing the 'What are you?' Encounters of Biracial in Individuals." In *The Multiracial Experience: Racial Borders as a Significant Frontier in Race Relations*, edited by Maria P.P. Root, 191-210. Thousand Oaks: Sage Publications, 1996.

On Being Mixed Race in a Mestizo-Dominated Community: The Ethnic Identity of Multiethnic Filipino Americans

Emilie Santos Tumale

Through the rising rates of intermarriage over recent decades, the Asian American community is not only growing in size but is also becoming increasingly multiethnic as more Asian Americans marry individuals outside of their own ethnicity or race. While Filipino Americans are generally marginalized within the Asian American and Pacific Islander (AAPI) community, they are nevertheless an ethnic group that expresses a significant amount of outmarriage—the act of marrying people outside of their ethnic group—within the AAPI community (Spickard 2001, 20). According to the 2010 United States Census, 25 percent of the Filipino American population identifies with another race or ethnic group. Furthermore, the amount of multiethnic or multiracial Filipinos has increased by about 67 percent between the years 2000 and 2010 while the entire Filipino American community has experienced a population growth of only 44 percent during that same time period (Hoeffel 2010). Although the Filipino American population is becoming increasingly mixed race, it in fact has been historically multiracial, as one of the first sizable Filipino American communities in the United States consisted of young Filipino men who often married women outside of their race (Burma 2012, 107). For this reason, it is important to acknowledge the mixed race Filipino American population in the United States.

This paper examines the ethnic identity of mixed race Filipino

Americans, or the offspring of one parent who self-identifies as Filipino and another parent who is not of Filipino ancestry. Most of the research in existence on multiethnic Filipinos primarily focuses on biracial white and Filipino Americans and biracial Mexican and Filipino Americans. In response to the current dearth of research and scholarship on this diverse population of mixed race Filipino Americans, this paper will contribute to scholarship on mixed race Asian Americans while also expanding upon perspectives within the disciplines of ethnic studies, Asian American studies, critical mixed race studies, and Filipino studies. While Filipino Americans and mixed race individuals both undergo relatively unique forms of racial identity development and racialization, multiethnic Filipinos consequently undergo such development as a result of both their Filipino ancestry and their racialization by monoethnic Filipino Americans. The intersectionality of their shared experience as ethnically Filipino, mixed race, and American-born cause them to develop their ethnic identity and *mestizo* consciousness in a manner that is different from other multiracial people who are not of Filipino ancestry (e.g., Anzaldúa 2012, 107). In order to examine the intersectionality of their Filipino ethnicity and their mixed race identity, this paper analyzes the case studies of multiethnic Filipinos of various ancestries in the context of their Filipino identity development, social identity, and approach to multiraciality.[2]

Research Methodology

Due to difficulties in finding a largely Filipino mixed race community outside of San Diego, California, this paper will draw its research upon the oral histories extracted from one hour interviews of five multiethnic individuals of Filipino descent between the ages of eighteen and twenty-five. All research subjects are affiliated with the author and University of California, Los Angeles. Each of them are of different ethnic backgrounds aside from their Filipino ancestry (African American, Thai, Caucasian,

---

[2] At the outset, I wish to acknowledge my own positionality vis-à-vis the topic of mixed race Filipino identity. As a monoethnic Filipino American, I recognize the historic complexity of racial mixture in the Philippines, and consequently of my own racial identity. At the same time, I view myself as an ally of the mixed race student movement.

Indian, and Mexican), and all have divergent academic backgrounds. While all of the interviewees are seeking a college education, each of their undergraduate experiences are unique in that they have pursued majors in different fields, such as English, political science, Asian American studies, and neuroscience.

Each of the interviewees is well acquainted with the author. Four out of the five interviewees met the author at the University of California, Los Angeles through Filipino American student organizations such as Pilipino Transfer Student Partnership (PTSP), Samahang Pilipino, and Pilipinos for Community Health (PCH). The remaining interviewee reached out to the author as soon as she discovered that they both were of Philippine ancestry during a week long residential program at UCLA. Each of the interviews were conducted individually at various venues within Los Angeles. Despite difficulties in organizing meeting times, the interviewees were pleased to share their experiences with the interviewer; however, this may be due to their friendship with the author or the author's positionality as a Filipino American college student.

Multiethnic Filipinos at a Glance: General Findings from the Case Studies

Mixed race Filipinos evidently have few common experiences with other mixed race Asian Americans in that they are multiethnic and they do not limit themselves to one ethnic category. However, those who are not of Caucasian ancestry have experiences that dramatically differ from the experiences of biracial Asian and white individuals who make up a significant portion of the mixed race Asian American population. Furthermore, multiethnic Filipinos have the shared experience of appearing as racially ambiguous more often than monoethnic Filipinos, an ethnic group that already has notable variability in physical ethnic markers such as skin tone, eye shape, and nose shape.

As United States colonization of the Philippines during the twentieth century has complicated the standardization of Filipino American culture, the development of positive perceptions for multiracial Filipino Americans of their Filipino ethnic identity largely depends on their experiences with extended family members and friends who are of Filipino descent rather than their exposure to Philippine traditions (De Jesús 2012, 7). Their need for a sense of camaraderie with other Filipino Americans is perhaps resultant of the salience of Philippine values such as *kapwa* (interrelatedness) and *utang na loob* (internal debt). Another way in which multiethnic Filipinos are unique to other mixed race Asian Americans is that most of them do not express the need to assert their Filipino identity in contrast to the multiethnic Asian American individuals who are represented in Murphy-Shigematsu's (2012) research. Rather than seeking to acquire fluency in the Tagalog dialect, which is characteristic of second generation Filipino Americans, multiethnic Filipinos either feel a symbolic cultural identity or they identify with the Philippine culture through family gatherings and food ways (Mendoza Strobel 1996). None of the interviewees have names that mark them as Filipino, nor have they felt the desire to change their names in order to mark them as Filipino—they were rather content with their respective last names and their Westernized first names. The remainder of this paper will further expand upon the shared experiences of these multiethnic Filipinos through the following motifs: racial and ethnic consciousness and "passing."

Racial and Ethnic Consciousness

To analyze the case studies of mixed race Filipino Americans, this paper draws from a variety of theoretical frameworks, including Kevin Nadal's Filipino racial and ethnic identity development model, Cynthia Nakashima's approach to multiraciality, and Christine Ijima Hall's interpretation of various factors affecting culture and racial identity.

Filipino Ethnic Identity Development

As a scholar in clinical psychology, Kevin Nadal has created a model to accurately illustrate the racial and ethnic identity development of Filipino Americans. The following is the sequence of phases that many Filipino Americans undergo in their lifetime, albeit to different degrees and at different rates: ethnic awareness, assimilation to the dominant culture, sociopolitical awakening, panethnic Asian American consciousness, ethnocentric realization, and introspection (Nadal 2011, 75). Because this theoretical framework may not accurately portray the experiences of multiethnic Filipino Americans, I utilize this model in order to assess the degree to which a mixed race Filipino American identifies as Filipino.

In other words, for the purpose of this study, if the interviewee did not appear to follow any of the phases in the model, then the subject would not be identified as one who considers being Filipino a salient aspect of his or her identity.

Based on their individual interviews, the subjects of this case study either did not follow Nadal's Filipino American Identity Development Model, or they did not reach the most advanced phase of ethnic identity development known as introspection—the embracing of all their racial identities as Filipino American, Asian American, and as a person of color. For several of them, entering college made them aware of their ethnic identity as mixed race or Filipino American for the first time. An individual of Black and Filipino descent recalled that he never had to think about his mixed race identity during his K-12 schooling experience, as he attended a private school and was of a middle class socioeconomic background (S. Tumale, in discussion with the author, May 10, 2013). This type of school setting was rather accepting of him, regardless of his race. Upon the start of his undergraduate career at UCLA, he saw for the first time in his life that students were likely to compartmentalize into different organizations based on their ethnicity. Because he did not feel like he could adequately claim a Filipino or Black identity, he joined Pilipinos for Community Health (an organization that serves the Filipino American community but is otherwise not culturally based) and the Mixed Student Union. An interviewee who identifies as Filipino and white also never thought about her racial identity as Filipino or as mixed race until entering the university. She recalls: "I don't think I've ever thought about [race]. The most surprising thing for me was when I got my first SPEAR [a Filipino American retention project] phone call: 'I'm your Filipino counselor!' . . . It was the first time I had to consider being Filipino as a significant factor" (In discussion with the author, May 14, 2013). Furthermore, since she is a majority-minority biracial Asian American, in that Filipinos are categorized as a minority group while whites are categorized as part of the majority, her upbringing in a geographical context with a significantly high concentration of racial minority groups has prevented her exclusion from white Americans, since she lacked the opportunity to interact with them while growing up (In discussion with the author, May 14, 2013).

One exception in this study is an individual who is of Thai and Filipino descent. His ability to "pass" as Filipino American has allowed him to explore his Filipino identity and learn more about Philippine and Filipino American culture through joining Pilipino Transfer Student Partnership at UCLA. His involvement in this student group has caused him to have a strong, ethnocentric identity as Filipino American. In reflecting upon what it means for him to be Filipino American, he states: "What it means to me is a sense of familiarity that I'm not alone in the world. And that's sort of the communal aspect. It's very hard to explain, but it reassures me that I'm not unique, as in I'm not a freak show. I mean, I have my different experiences, but there are people who can understand those shared experiences . . . It's a way of connection, and it's a way of familiarity (In discussion with the author, May 15, 2013). Although this interviewee has not grown up with a salient Filipino ethnic identity, he currently feels a sense of belonging to Filipinos regardless of blood quantum. Even with his multicultural upbringing as Thai, Filipino, and American, he asserts that he has shared experiences with monoracial Filipino Americans.

Symbolic Identity

In analyzing the experiences of mixed race Mexican and white Americans living in Santa Clara County, Tomás R. Jiménez (2004) proposes that mixed race Mexican and white Americans often express a sense of symbolic ethnic identity if they feel detached from their Mexican heritage. Jiménez defines symbolic identity as "a nostalgic allegiance to the culture of the immigrant generation" and asserts that it "stems from their limited experience and knowledge of their ethnic background" (2004, 84-94). Because his research is on biracial Mexicans and whites, this form of ethnic identity is not entirely applicable to multiethnic Filipino Americans, in that Filipino American communities and culture are not as accessible to them as Mexican American communities and enclaves are to mixed race Mexican Americans. Nevertheless, a third generation Filipino and white interviewee feels rather acculturated. In talking about her and her Filipino extended family, she states: "I have a lot of cousins . . . They're all second and third generation, too. None of them are from the Philippines . . . I always feel like we are very Americanized—well, I'm definitely American—and they are too, just because we lived here, we grew up here, [and] none of us went to the Philippines" (Santos Tumale, in discussion with the author, May 15, 2013).

Unlike second-generation monoracial Filipino Americans, this interviewee expresses less cultural ties with the Philippines as a homeland. Her generational status and her identity as mixed race have allowed her to have a symbolic Filipino American identity. Meanwhile, the continuous growth of the Filipino American community through high rates of intermarriage and immigration make the Philippine culture distinctly salient in the United States. Even with the subsequent generations of Filipinos born in the United States, the ethnic identity of future generations of Filipino Americans will unlikely become symbolic unless they were to pass as other races or start following the traditional model of assimilation (Zhou 2004, 29-37).

Multiracial Consciousness

All mixed race individuals have their own way of defining their racial identity. While there is a multiracial movement that is currently gaining momentum in the United States, mixed race individuals have variable investment in or even knowledge of this movement. Nevertheless, there is a significant presence of mixed race representation in academia through the departments of ethnic studies and mixed race studies, and there are organizations created by and for mixed race individuals in college campuses and in the community at large. Within the multiracial movement, Cynthia Nakashima (1992) asserts that there are three different but not mutually exclusive objectives: to struggle for inclusion and legitimacy in traditional ethnic communities, to shape a common identity and agenda among multiracial people, and to break down dominant racial ideologies to create cross-cultural communities (1992, 79-97). The majority of the interviewees were of the first and/ or third categories.

One example among the interviewees is a multiethnic individual of Filipino and Indian descent. His initial response to the author asking him how he identifies himself is the following: "I identify as a mutt. I don't stick to one race. If someone asks, 'What are you?' I just say half Indian, half Filipino" (In discussion with the author, May 12, 2013). While all interviewees had their own way of stating their ethnic identity (most were straightforward), this individual was the only one to specifically identify as mixed, even using a term that is particular to mixed breed animals and is therefore offensive to some mixed race people. While he generally feels accepted in Filipino American groups on campus, he has expressed a sense of angst from being biracial; a feeling that is shared among multiracial subjects from previous studies who argue that biraciality is a deficit and undesirable trait (Root 2001, 62).

The Indian and Filipino American interviewee recalled experiences of not being fully accepted by his peers in middle school. Although he had an elder brother as a role model and positive influence at the time, his classmates used his biracial identity to insult him and mark him as different. While he had a degree of positive interactions with his relatives, he found that even his extended family looked down upon him for being mixed race and for not being "fully" Filipino or "fully" Indian. His phenotypic appearance as African American or Mexican American challenges the Model Minority Stereotype, for he appears to be neither Filipino American nor Indian American. It was not until he transferred to UCLA and obtained his bachelor's degree that his relatives began to view him positively: as a "good Filipino" or a "good Indian" who managed to get an education" (In discussion with the author, May 12, 2013).

Overall, the interviewees acknowledged their multiple ethnic backgrounds, but did not feel welcome to solely claim one ethnic identity. As a result of society's continuing notions of culture being passed down biologically, mixed race Filipinos raised with multiple cultures are perceived to have "diluted" Filipino identities—even if they are monoracial Filipino Americans who grow up without much exposure to their culture or to their extended family. For instance, a mixed race Mexican and *mestizo* Filipino American interviewee perceives herself in the following manner: "I identify myself as a mixed person. I don't feel right saying I'm Mexican or I'm Filipino. I say I'm both all the time" (In discussion with the author, May 14, 2013). Furthermore, because she has a difficult time identifying with the monoracial Filipino American community, her notion of being Filipino refers to her culture and her family history. She elaborates:

> The richest history that I know of, that is very dear to me,
> is my Filipino history, because it's very detailed and there's
> proof behind it . . . Our oral history has been passed

down generation to generation. Even in old Filipino maps, there's [our] territory. Even when I go to the Philippines, everyone knows who I am. They know [my family]. Even though we're not rich or anything . . . back then, we used to own almost all of it. I feel like that's a kind of history that I don't want to let go of. [B]eing Filipino means preserving that history, and probably preserving the oral history. But I can't say I've adopted the traditions. I don't do the blessing thing [*pagmano*]; I don't do a lot of [things] (In discussion with the author, May 14, 2013).

Because she does not claim to have Filipino ancestry through her lack of Filipino cultural knowledge, this interviewee expresses ethnic pride over the class privilege her ancestors had after the Spanish American War. Her Filipino ethnic identity is linked to history and culture rather than racial appearance simply because she does not phenotypically appear to be Filipino, as with the rest of her ancestors on her Filipino father's side. Despite being of two ancestries that embody a sense of *mestizaje* (mixed ancestry historically linked to Spanish colonialism), she has a rather unique notion of race and culture (De Jesús 2004, 219-52). In response to the question "Do you think Filipinos are innately mixed?" she responded:

In my perspective, Filipino is not a race; it's a culture . . . I feel that Filipinos are not a race. I don't know about innately mixed; they don't exist. We're just a compilation of a group that was conquered and welcomed different types of people. There are Filipinos that look very different. Some look African, some look Spanish, [and] some look Chinese. I don't feel like I'm any race, since Mexicans are the same. There's no such thing as a Mexican. If you want to get technical, a Mexican is a Spaniard mixed with a native (In discussion with the author, May 14, 2013).

Rather than seeing Filipino as a mixed race, she sees it as a pluralistic community that is diverse in other races and cultures. She even extends this analogy to her conception of Mexicans. Ironically, she categorizes them as a mix between the colonizer and the indigenous population. It is interesting that she does not apply this racial hierarchy to the Philippines, which also had its share of race mixing between Spaniards and indigenous Filipinos.

Racial Markers and "Passing"
Racially Ambiguous Physical Appearances

The notion of "passing" involves the ability for an individual with a somewhat racially ambiguous appearance to shift his or her reference point from one race to another (Daniel 1992). Historically speaking, this allowed biracial whites and African Americans to integrate with the white community before the Civil Rights Movement (Daniel 1992, 91-107). In the case of this research study, multiracial Filipino Americans are most often perceived to be Latino. It is rare for a multiethnic Filipino to pass as Filipino. One counter example based on this study would be an individual who is Thai and Filipino American. Due to his monoracial identity as Southeast Asian (the Philippines is geographically part of Southeast Asia), he has been able to easily integrate with the Filipino American community at UCLA. In general, his phenotypic features—particularly his dark skin—have allowed him to be welcomed in both of his ethnic communities. He elaborates:

> I look Filipino and I look Thai, and that visual cue automatically makes people accept [me], and it puts that first impression. Before I even speak, that's the first impression: *This guy might be . . .* and automatically there's that connection there. I have some cousins that are light skinned, and they're treated a bit differently because of their skin color. Like, *Oh those are the white kids*. They're mixed, but because they're light skinned, they're perceived as white (In discussion with the author, May 15, 2013).

This interviewee's ability to pass as Filipino or as Thai has allowed him to be more welcomed by his relatives and has allowed him to practice his multicultural identity as Thai, Filipino, and American without objection from them. While he was never granted the opportunity to become fluent in Thai or Tagalog, he possesses positive cultural values and he even expresses faith in both Buddhism and Catholicism. His ability to navigate both ethnic communities has provided him with a rich ethnic identity development—what some mixed race individuals call "the best of both worlds"—even as he wrestles with his identity of being American since he is second generation Thai and Filipino.

Westernized Names and American Assimilation

Due to the limited sample size and the unique family histories of each of the multiethnic Filipino interviewees, all of them had names that did not mark them as Filipino. Each of them have Western or biblical first names, have non-Filipino last names due to their non-Filipino patrilineage, and have middle names that are not the same as their Filipino mother's maiden name—a typical ethnic marker for Filipinos and Filipino Americans. The reason why most of the interviewees did not have Filipino names (including their middle names) was because their parents wanted them to assimilate to American society. An interviewee of Caucasian and Filipino descent recalled her parents being "adamant about keeping [her] name as American as possible. They wanted to have classic names, so it wasn't that [she] was signifying [herself] as something—just as a regular person" (In discussion with the author, May 14, 2013). In turn, her name is not racially ambiguous in any matter. Her and her parents consider her to be "American" though it is possible that in turn she is also intended to be as white as possible. Meanwhile, an individual of Indian and Filipino descent also appreciates that he has a first name that does not mark him as a person of color. Unlike some of his Indian cousins, he is thankful to not have a name that can allow people to racially insult him (In discussion with the author, May 16, 2013).

The interviewees' American names, however, contrasted with their racially ambiguous phenotypic features. An individual of Mexican, Filipino, Chinese, and Anglo ancestry feels that her name and her appearance confuses others and leads to a sense of "misidentification," which can be a challenge for her when she tries to assert a certain ethnic identity, such as a Mexican applying for a Latina scholarship or a person of color who does well in a science class" (see Burma 2012, 107). An individual of Thai and Filipino descent also perceives his name to not align with his ethnic identity since his last name originates from his Thai father's stepfather who is of Italian descent. However, he sees his name as an advantage because it causes others to initially perceive him as white. He elaborates: "My last name is actually Italian, and so people can't really tell. I'm sure when people see my resumé, they see [my name] and they think of a white guy" (In discussion with the author, May 15, 2013).

An interviewee of Black and Filipino descent has this similar experience of liking his name, which ethnically marks him as African American. He elaborates: "Some people think my name is really Black. Because I don't look 100 percent Black, sometimes people will wonder about it until I reveal my mixed heritage to them and then they understand" (In discussion with the author, May 10, 2013).

Like most mixed race individuals, the apparent mismatch between their names and their physical appearances causes outsiders to somewhat police the racial and ethnic identities of multiethnic Filipino Americans. However, unlike other mixed race Asian Americans who desire to assert their ethnic identity through modifying their names or emphasizing parts of their names that mark them as Asian (Nakashima 2001, 111-120), the multiethnic Filipinos in this study do not seek to change their names. Furthermore, none of the interviewed mixed race Filipinos in this study expressed any interest in learning more about their Philippine culture in the same manner that monoracial and second generation Filipino Americans do, such as by learning how to speak Tagalog or by joining large-scale Filipino American organizations on campus.

Limitations

While the multiethnic Filipinos who have participated in this study have a multitude of shared experiences in terms of their acceptance (or lack thereof) in the Filipino community, ranging from their strong connections with their Filipino relatives to their racially ambiguous appearances and their cultural practices, there are several variables that prevent one from making accurate generalizations of mixed race Filipinos and even the co-ethnic communities of the interviewees. The sample size for this study is limited in terms of its size and the demographic it represents: mixed race college students in the Los Angeles area. Some of the interviewees in this case study had Filipino family histories that greatly differ from the

Filipino American community at large. For instance, the family history of an interviewee of Filipino and Mexican descent is unique not only to Mexipinos, but also to Filipinos Americans in general. Similarly, a Black and Filipino American interviewee's decision to utilize a nickname that is not a racial identifier is not connected to his desire to assert his Asian identity. In addition, it was difficult to find an interviewee who was half white and half second-generation Filipino, as the non-white interviewees were multiracial second-generation Filipino Americans. As demonstrated in other studies on mixed race individuals, one must consider the socioeconomic background, geographic context, level of academic achievement, and other factors in order to investigate the ethnic and racial identity formations of mixed race Filipinos. However, the aim of case studies is not to find accurate sample populations but to explore individual cases. In this way, this paper has demonstrated some of the diversity within the Filipino American community, while also identifying some of the shared experiences of mixed race Filipinos.

Lastly, it would be useful for others to add to this research on mixed race Filipino Americans. The original intent of this study was to investigate differences between mixed race Filipino Americans of different ethnicities other than white and Mexican. While this research showed similarities between the multiethnic Filipinos in this study, it presents perhaps a misleading view that multiethnic Filipino Americans do not identify with the Filipino American community as a result of their experiences differing from other second-generation Filipino Americans.

Conclusion

Multiethnic Filipinos present various similarities and differences with mixed race individuals who are not of Filipino ancestry. Similarities include ethnic identity development based on group inclusion or exclusion, racial ambiguity, and the effects of names and phenotype on their racialization. Nevertheless, mixed race Filipinos have unique experience from other mixed race Asian Americans due to their phenotypic features that sometimes allow them to pass as monoracial, but not particularly Asian. As ethnic markers, their names also have the potential to separate them from other Filipinos, who often possess traditionally Spanish, Chinese, or indigenous Filipino surnames. Paradoxically, although Filipinos are a pluralistic society to the extent that non-Filipinos categorize them as "innately mixed," Filipinos do express a degree of racial ideology that not only values whiteness but also Spanish *mestizaje* as well. Depending on one's particular biracial background, mixed Filipino Americans either blend in well with the community, are rejected, or are exoticized by monoethnic Filipinos. Due to the current marginality—or sometimes spectacle—of multiethnic Filipino Americans, it is important to acknowledge their mixed race identities while also welcoming them as an integral part of the Filipino American community.

Bibliography

Anzaldúa, Gloria. *Borderlands/La Frontera: The New Mestiza.* San Francisco, CA: Aunt Lute Books, 1987.

Burma, John H. "Research Note on the Measurement of Interracial Marriage." *American Journal of Sociology 57,* no. 6 (May 1952): 587-89.

Daniel, G. Reginald. "Passers and Pluralists: Subverting the Racial Divide." In *Racially Mixed People in America*, edited by Maria P. P. Root, 91-107. Newbury Park, CA: Sage Publications, 1992.

De Jesús, Melinda L. "Liminality and Mestiza Consciousness in Lynda Barry's 'One Hundred Demons'." *MELUS Filipino American Literature* 29, no. 1(Spring 2004): 219-52.

Guevarra Jr., Rudy. "Burritos and Bagoong: Mexipinos and Multiethnic Identity in San Diego, California." In *Crossing Lines: Race and Mixed Race Across Geohistorical Divide*, edited by Marc Coronado, Rudy P. Guevarra Jr., Jeffrey Moniz, and Laura F. Szanto. Lanham, 73-95. MD: AltaMira Press, 2005.

Iikima-Hall, C. C., and Trude I. Cooke Turner. "The Diversity of Biracial Individuals: Asian-White and Asian-Minority Biracial Identity." In *The Sum of Our Parts: Mixed Heritage Asian Americans,* edited by Teresa Williams-León & Cynthia L. Nakashima. Philadelphia: Temple University Press, 2001.

Jiménez, Tomas R. "Negotiating Ethnic Boundaries: Mexican Americans and Ethnic Identity in the United States." *Ethnicities* 4, no. 1 (March 2004): 75-97.

Murphy-Shigematsu, Stephen. *When Half is Whole: Multiethnic Asian American Identities.* Stanford, CA: Stanford University Press, 2012.

Nadal, Kevin L. *Filipino American Psychology: A Handbook of Theory, Research, and Clinical Practice.* Hoboken, NJ: Wiley, 2011.

Nakashima, Cynthia L. "Voices from the Movement: Approaches to Multiraciality." In *The Multicultural Experience: Racial Borders as a Significant Frontier in Race Relations,* edited by Maria P. P. Root, 79-97. Thousand Oaks, CA: Sage Publications, 1995.

Nakashima, Daniel A. "A Rose by Any Other Name: Names, Multiracial/Multiethnic People, and the Politics of Identity." In *The Sum of Our Parts: Mixed Heritage Asian Americans,* edited by Teresa Williams-León & Cynthia L. Nakashima. Philadelphia: Temple University Press, 2001.

Sohn, S. H. Review of *American Tropics: Articulating Filipino America,* by Allan. P. Isaac. *MELUS* 32, no. 2 (June 2007): 190-93.

Spickard, Paul R. and Rowena Fong. "Pacific Islander Americans and Multiethnicity: A Vision of America's Future?" *Social Forces* 58, no. 4 (1995): 1365-383.

Strobel, Leny M. "'Born-Again Filipino': Filipino American Identity and Asian Panethnicity." *Amerasia Journal* 22, no. 2 (1996): 31-53.

Williams, Teresa K., and Michael C. Thornton. "Social Construction of Ethnicity Versus Personal Experience: The case of Afro-Amerasians." In *Contemporary Asian America: A Multidisciplinary Reader,* edited by M. Zhou & J. Gatewood. New York: New York University Press, 2007.

Zhou, Min. "Are Asian Americans becoming 'White'?" *Contexts* 3, no. 1 (2004): 29-37.

The Blonde Hmong Phenomenon

Fuemeng Jimmy Fang

Is that your natural hair color? Did you dye it? What are you? These are merely but a few of a multitude of questions I personally experience when I first meet someone. It can get tiresome at times, always having to identify myself and explaining who I am. In the Hmong community, there is a rare recessive phenotype, which exhibits a lighter or blonde hair color. I am one of these few individuals who possess this rare phenotype and though it is widely known in the Hmong community, it is also widely unknown at the same time. This particular phenotype discourages people from partaking in cultural events such as beauty pageants and parallels to the multiracial experience, where people feel judged or discriminated based solely on how they look. Though this idea emerges from two different phenomena, I will primarily focus on the blonde Hmong phenomenon. Through narratives, I hope to shed light on the discourses that are brought up when these stereotypes are bothered or challenged in the Hmong community and the connections between language, culture and phenotype. From here I will bridge phenotype with the parallel experiences of marginalization and operations of power that apply to both monoethnics and multiethnics.

Background

Certain terms are used in the Hmong community to describe individuals who possess this recessive phenotype. Though many terms are used the prevalent ones are *mekas dawb* (*"white person"*) or *menyuam mekas dawb* (*"white person's child"*) and *menyuam pojnxtoog plaubhau daj qhovmuag xiav* (blonde-haired blue-eyed demon child). There is a negative connotation that is attached to each of these terms as well as a tendency to hyper focus on other races while overlooking the Hmong aspect. For instance, though the first term, *mekas dawb* or *menyuam mekas dawb*, specifically refers to a White person it can also be interchanged with other races (e.g., white, Black, Hispanic and some other Asian backgrounds).

In ancient times, the Hmong people had blonde hair and blue eyes. Through the use of phenotype as marker, the Chinese were able to identify the Hmong. As the Hmong migrated over time out of China and into other regions, the phenotype became lost and less frequent. The Hmong people have no country to call their own; the Hmong culture remains in flux because as the next generation arrives, young people will experience the conditions of their own lives, define them, and respond to them. During this process, the Hmong will produce unique cultural forms and practices that become the expressions and products of their own experiences. These factors including phenotype all play a significant role in the decisions that the next generation will make and essentially pass onto the next generation. As a result, the next generation will undoubtedly feel conflict and obligation to choose between what to focus on more or less and in doing so will end up on the crossroads of what they value more. It will be up to the next generation to uplift and guide the Hmong community.

Methodology

For this study I will be looking at Hmong communities in the United States, and more specifically in California. I will be focusing on Hmong individuals who exhibit a lighter or blonde hair color. My study is substantiated mainly by qualitative data. This is due to the fact that there is very little documented data or research done on this recessive phenotype in the Hmong community. Therefore, I will be drawing from personal interviews and other resources that deal with the phenotypical aspect of the multiracial experience. Figure 1 displays the survey I designed to address the interviewees' experiences as someone who identifies as Hmong with the recessive phenotype and whether they have competed or thought about competing in cultural events such as Hmong beauty pageants.

Name:
Age:
Gender:

Hmong Phenotype Study

Hi my name is Jimmy Fang and I'm a graduating senior at UCLA studying Asian American Studies. I'm conducting a phenotype study that explores the split between phenotype and culture in the Hmong community. This regards more specifically the recessive phenotype that exhibits the lighter or blonde hair color among Hmong individuals. Essentially I'm working on shedding light on the discourses that are brought up when these stereotypes are bothered or challenged in the Hmong community especially with Hmong beauty pageants.

*Below are some of the basic questions, but feel free to expand as much as you want.

1. How do you identify yourself?
2. How many other Hmong people do you know that exhibit the same or similar phenotype (lighter/blonde hair color) as you? Anyone else within your family?
3. Growing up did you know or feel differently than other Hmong people? Did you feel like you didn't belong or felt discriminated based on how you looked?
4. Have you ever competed in a Mr. or Miss Hmong Pageant? If you haven't, did you ever consider doing one?
5. Have you thought about competing in a Mr. or Miss Hmong Pageant but decided not to due to your phenotype?
6. Would it be okay for me to contact you to follow up on these questions?
7. Any other thoughts/stories/comments/questions?

Thank you!

Figure 1. Hmong Phenotype Study Survey

My vision was to compile the theories from readings with personal interviews including my own experiences to exemplify the parallel experiences to multiraciality. My study is framed as three separate episodes that are based off of King-O'Riain's book, *Pure Beauty*. Each episode will comprise the experiences of each individual, who I surveyed for this research. Through word of mouth, email, and social media, I connected with Gloria Lee and Sauci Xiong and followed up with both via the same modes of communication.

As with any study, there are limitations that I could not change or control: one being the time constraint of the quarter system, thus limiting the scope of my study; the second being the diversity of potential interviewees due to the limited access to potential interviewees who possesses the recessive phenotype. The survey in itself is a limitation due to its ambiguity in respect to open-ended questions. The narratives that are brought up can be broad or not necessarily be aligned with the other narratives. Again, due to the lack of academic research about my topic, I looked to alternative forms of research such as qualitative data and observations that included multimedia as well as other research done in communities beyond the Hmong community. Essentially, I will be looking into pictures, videos, social media, and blogs in the context of my study from a meso-level analysis.

Beyond the Judgment

Gloria[1] in Figure 2 identifies both as a Hmong American and someone who exhibits the recessive phenotype. Three out of the seven siblings from her family exhibit the blonde hair color such as her sister donning traditional Hmong clothes at an early age in Figure 3. Growing up, she knew at least a dozen others Hmong people who have this trait.

Figure 2. Gloria Lee Headshot.

Figure 3. Younger Maicy Lee (Sister, Left) and Younger Gloria Lee (Right).

Gloria shared with me two incidents from her past surrounding her hair color: one during her early childhood and another during her early teenage years:

> I didn't think my hair color was an issue until I was four. My family sold fabric at the swap meets and I went along to help. Elder Hmong women who came to buy fabric would scold me to not touch anything they planned to buy because I was a "menyuam pojnxtoog plaubhau daj, qhovmuag xiav" (blonde-haired blue-eyed demon child). I don't have blue eyes, by the way. My eyes are a lighter shade of brown than most other Hmong people. That was the first time I felt rejected by people of my own ethnic background and realized that my hair color was going to be a trait that people would make into an issue. When I got to my early teens I was often mistaken as a "gangster" because it was trendy for rebellious Hmong girls to bleach or highlight their hair to lighter colors so I often got the stink eye without doing anything. (In discussion with the author, May, 21, 2014).

Guevarra (2003) points out that, "Language is the way in which we define ourselves and the world around us. It is a means to empower or oppress, and is important to the issue of race relations. With regards to identity, language has always been reformed with the times to accommodate each varying generation and the terms they use to describe themselves" (73-96). When these cultural terms are used from such an early age, it can condition young individuals to feel rejected; therefore, it is important to address the issue when it occurs. Furthermore, Williams (1992) articulates that languages, "depending upon who view[s] them, ... [are] perceived, defined, and treated quite differently" (1992, 290), which can be attributed to the multiracial experience, where one is being judged and discriminated against especially from their very own communities.

When asked about whether she ever competed in or thought about competing in Hmong beauty pageants, Gloria said:

> No, I never competed in a Miss Hmong Pageant. My family owns a business and we were regularly asked to sponsor the contestants so competing would have been bad for business and since the community is very closely knitted, many people would assume unfair judging if I was to win, which will also lead to bad business and the end of many relationships (In discussion with the author, May 21, 2014).

From these experiences, I asked Gloria whether she did not compete because of her phenotype and she said, "No. I cried for a whole afternoon about being hated and judged due to my hair color when I was four. I also decided after that long cry, when I was four, that I was above all the judgment and hatred, so I never let any of that judgment bother me anymore" (In discussion with the author, May 21, 2014). What Gloria experienced from an early age mirrors Williams' (1992) comment, that "the social effects of [individuals'] physical appearances on their ethnic identity choices [are] important, but not definitive" (1992, 292) and demonstrates where physical appearance can play an important role in ethnic identity development among racially mixed people. There is a sense of essence that is shaped from Gloria's childhood, one that has given her the agency to identify who she is with confidence and goes hand in hand to embody true empowerment.

Miss Hmong

Sauci[2] in Figure 4 identifies as a twenty-first century American Hmong girl living in California, post-Vietnam war. Among her friends and family, she knows fifteen other individuals who possessed the recessive phenotype. Sauci exhibits the blonde hair color from an early age in Figure 5.

Figure 4. Sauci Xiong Headshot

Figure 5. Younger Sauci Xiong.

Through survey, Sauci shared with me about her past experiences growing up with the recessive phenotype:

> I never felt discriminated in fact felt more like I fit in since I grew up in a heavily populated Caucasian area. I knew I was different but it didn't bother me. I used to Hmong dance. One year, my sister and I (she has yellow hair too) had to dye our hair to "match" the other girls. I didn't like the idea. By the date we were supposed to perform, it faded back to yellow. I haven't dyed my hair since then.

My hair is a part of me and is what makes me unique (In discussion with the author, May 22, 2014).

With a positive outlook, it is easy to see Lim's (2008) perspective on how, "beauty pageants have been especially fruitful sites for examining how youth make meaning out of their lives, for the young participants have acted as representatives of family power as well as representatives of community, nation, race, and ethnicity" (2008, 215-216). When asked about whether she ever competed in or thought about competing in Miss Hmong Pageants, Sauci said:

I have done multiple Hmong and American pageants. For Hmong: Little Miss Hmong, Miss Hmong Merced, Miss Waterfest, Miss Hmong California, Miss Hmong International. I loved doing them. It was so much fun for my family and I. Going into pageants, all other contestants felt they had an advantage over me because they have black hair which is favored in Hmong pageants as being the idealistic Asian beauty. My mom has told me to dye my hair black multiple times for pageants. I always decline (In discussion with the author, May 22, 2014).

As Spickard (1997) points out, "Physical appearance, however, does not completely determine one's identity" (1997, 45). For Sauci, her phenotype did not stop her from competing in the Miss Hmong Pageants but instead she embraced who she was. This weaves into the idea of being accepted into a community that is at the same time already struggling to be accepted based solely on culture. King-O'Riain (2006) further argues that, "Because the queen is a living symbol of a collective identity, she must embody the collective she wishes to represent. In this instance . . . it weaves race into the equation so that the symbol (queen) must also be racialized. When the queen is multiracial not only is the race of the symbol shifted, but so is the symbol itself" (2006, 79). What arose from this is the issue of how race plays a role in determining authenticity and essentially came down to what the community wants. As a result, pageants are structured in a way that allows the entire community the right to comment on candidates as a way to appease everyone. There are two definitions that come to mind: the community definition and the outside media image of beauty and it is in these pageants where these standards of beauty are affirmed and enforced. Just like with multiracial candidates where the race of the symbol is shifted, so is the symbol itself. This parallels to Hmong beauty pageant candidates who possess the recessive phenotype, competing to gain the acceptance of the community and to be authenticated by them as a representative of the community. As someone who competed in these pageants and won, Sauci represents the counter imperative to the notion that being different phenotypically makes one disadvantageous as well as breaking the social norm of what a Miss Hmong should look like.

All Natural

I[3] identify as a Hmong American as seen in Figure 6. Growing up in Fresno, I knew very few people who exhibited the recessive phenotype outside of my family, including my immediate and extended family. Figure 7 captures a younger version of myself along with my younger sister who does not possess the recessive phenotype.

Figure 6. Jimmy Fang Headshot.

Figure 7. Younger Nancy Fang (Sister, Left) and Younger Jimmy Fang (Right).

From an early age, I would hear stories from my parents on how I got the hair color genes from my grandfather on my dad's side of the family. My mom used to have the recessive hair color when she was younger but it faded as she reached puberty. For me, it was a different story:

> I think for the longest time, it never occurred to me that I was different until I was around five when I started to go to school. There it became clear that I looked different than other Hmong people and as I went through the K-12 system, it was obvious that I was the only Hmong person who looked the way I did. A part of me never really fit in with the other Hmong kids growing up and I came to believe it was because of my hair color. I knew this especially when I went out with my family to the grocery store or restaurant; people would talk about me under their breath. When I do hear it, it usually goes into questions about whether I'm adopted, whether I'm mixed, whether I dyed my hair, or whether I'm Hmong (In discussion with the author, May 24, 2014).

Valverde (1992) argues that among many communities, "Community prejudice may not be blatant, but subtle words can also hurt" (1992, 158). I definitely say that these forms of microaggressions from within my own community turned me bitter and I became a "Hmong hater" into my teenage years. However as I entered my first year of college at UCLA, I was presented with an interesting opportunity that would disrupt the discourse of Hmong beauty pageants:

Yes, I competed in the 2009 Mr. Hmong Pageant that was organized by CSU Fresno's Hmong Student Union (HMSA). This was their first time putting on such an event and was also probably one of the first to do so in the region. Going into this competition, I thought I had a clear vision of what it was trying to accomplish, promoting higher education via college educated male role models for the community; but, as the weeks approached and the event ensued, it became clear that the beauty pageant became a beauty pageant in the end. Out of all the contestants, I was the only one who had the recessive phenotype. Ultimately, the pageant broke down to pure aesthetics, where we, the contestants, were being judged based on how we walk down a catwalk wearing casual clothes, formal clothes and our traditional Hmong clothes. During the times where we would answer questions, it was unclear if we were to answer in Hmong or English but I chose to interchange between the two or "Hmonglish." It was tough because a part of me felt during the whole time, I was trying to prove my "Hmongness" to the judges who at that time was a former Ms. Hmong beauty pageant winner, a Hmong rap artist, and a Hmong college counselor (In discussion with the author, May 24, 2014).

It was not until after participating in the Mr. Hmong Pageant that I realized how much phenotype mattered and through a multiracial lens, the similarities were uncanny. Essentially I told myself that I would never do another one again. King-O'Riain (2006) substantiated this claim by saying how, "racial and ethnic beauty pageants highlight how race is about the process of marking the body as different in terms of physicality—for example, skin color, eyes, hair, and body shape [and] in the end, is in large part about judging appearance, in which race plays a large role, and not necessarily the person in her entirety" (2006, 76-77). One blogger adds that, "The winner and runner ups are supposed to be 'role models' . . . However, the judges don't even care about the candidate's background. In fact, it's pretty much like what the title says a 'Beauty Pageant' where the candidates are judged based on their physical appearance and how they present themselves by their attire outfit and evening gown" (Mystics of Life, 2014). Tiffany Vang (2014) mentions that, "Many may say that the Hmong Beauty Pageant is not based on looks, but to '*saib leej twj muaj peev xwm*,' which means 'to test one's ability/ capability.'" Yet judges are not assessing these pageant candidates based on their resumé, background, struggles, service experience in the Hmong community, ambitions or dreams. Instead it is based solely on one's presentation in their evening gown, creative Hmong clothes, and a question that tests one's Hmong language capability. Underneath it all, the phenotype criteria shapes who wins. Even so, the notion to challenge the stereotypes in an arena built upon phenotypes and culture is but the first step toward developing a critical consciousness in addressing these issues in the larger community.

Conclusion

In light of one's phenotype, no matter how beautiful or unique, it is easy for one to be blinded by one's ignorance. In reality, marginalization and operations of power affect both monoethnics and multiethnics at the meso-level, which span from the individual to the family and to the larger community. The parallels between multiracial individuals and those with the recessive phenotype is depicted via multiple passing where "the individual can easily pass and blend in and out of their cultures and ethnicities, as well as others not associated with their backgrounds. This ability to transcends one's own physical appearance and outsider expectations is the result of multiple passing" (Guevarra 2003, 84). Yet the connection of experiences goes beyond the physicality and adds depth to both culture and identity. To make matters more complicated, I, along with Gloria, Sauci and many other second-generation children, are already left with shards of a shattered mirror of our culture. The very search for the voices of my people can sometimes counter-intuitively reinforce this fragmentation because it forces me to focus on the specific histories of individuals that have been examined in isolation from larger social, economic and political contexts. Beauty pageants will continue to be an avenue where "Asian American communities can invoke or reinterpret their past, which can also signal future directions for the community" (Lim 2008, 217). In this way, it will work towards articulating alternative cultural practices to counter the dominant discourse. To better understand the connection between culture and phenotype requires me to not only view monoethnics and multiethnics as two opposing forces but rather as two pieces that compliment one another. In doing so, it will allow me to slowly reflect and appreciate who I am as I put the shattered mirror of my culture back together.

Notes

1   Gloria Lee was born in West Covina, California but her parents moved to Merced at the demand of the Lee Clan. There she lived until 2005 where she came to UCLA and finished her undergraduate degree three years later. She moved back home for two months and got a job as a lab technician in Los Angeles where she has worked since the fall of 2008. Currently, Gloria is the quality control team lead at a facility that provides specialty testing of blood borne pathogens. For the past nine years, she has moved and lived all over Los Angeles County but is currently in Long Beach now and going to school at CSU Dominguez Hills for a certificate license in medical technology (CLS) and working full time.

2   Sauci Xiong grew up in the city of Turlock, California where there were very few Hmong people then eventually moved to the rural parts of Merced where the Hmong there were only a handful. Her dad is an only child so she did not go to a lot of Hmong parties and still does not. A majority of her friends growing up were of all nationalities. Currently, Sauci is residing in Fresno, where the Hmong population as well as culture is very different. Sauci guesses that she would be experiencing the "real Hmong environment" for the first time and is currently a senior at Fresno State majoring in Recreation Administration - Commercial Recreation.

3   I, Fuemeng Jimmy Fang, was born and raised in Fresno, California. Growing up in one of the largest Hmong communities in the United States shaped how I saw the world through the lens as both the eldest son of a Hmong family and as a second generation Hmong American. Whether it be going to Hmong parties on the weekend, helping my cousins move, or doing soul calling ceremonies every now and then, it was all part of being part of the Fang Clan. I graduated from Hoover High School in 2009 then went to attend UCLA in the fall of 2009 where I completed my undergraduate degree in the spring of 2014.

Bibliography

Coronado, M., Rudy P. Guevarra Jr., Jeffrey Moniz, Laura F. Szanto, eds. *Crossing lines: Race and Mixed Race Across Geohistorical Divide.* Lanham, MD: AltaMira Press, 2005.

Guevarra Jr., Rudy P. *Becoming Mexipino: Multiethnic Identities and Communities in San Diego.* Piscataway, NJ: Rutgers University Press, 2012.

King-O'Riain, Rebecca C. *Pure Beauty: Judging Race in Japanese American Beauty Pageants.* Minneapolis: University of Minnesota Press, 2006.

Lim, Shirley J. "Asian American Youth Culture". *Journal of Asian American Studies* 11, no. 2 (June 2008): 211-28.

Mystics of Life (2013). Controversy Topic: Hmong Beauty Pageants. Retrieved from Web.

Spickard, Paul R. "What must I be? Asian Americans and the Question of Multiethnic Identity". *Amerasia Journal* 23, no. 1 (1997): 43-60.

Valverde, KLC. "From Dust to Gold: The Vietnamese Amerasian Experience." In *Racially Mixed People in* America, edited by Maria P. P. Root, 144-161. Newbury Park, CA: Sage Publications, 1992.

Vang, Tiffany. "Hmong Beauty Pageants: Empowering or Not?" I Am Hmong Beauty (blog). January 31, 2013. https://www.facebook.com/ iamhmongbeauty/photos/hmong-beauty-pageants-empowering-or -notby-tiffany-vangits-quite-hard-to-know-wha/385144531582079/.

Williams, Teresa K. "Prism Lives: Identity of Binational Amerasians." In *Racially Mixed People in* America, edited by Maria P. P. Root, 280-304. Newbury Park, CA: Sage Publications, 1992.

Appendix: Surveys

Name: Gloria Lee
Age: Twenty-nine
Gender: Female

Hmong Phenotype Study

1. How do you identify yourself?
    Hmong American
2. How many other Hmong people do you know that exhibit the same or similar phenotype (lighter/blonde hair color) like you? Anyone else within your family?
    Out of seven kids in my family, three have blonde/red hair. Growing up, I have personally known at least at least a dozen other Hmong people who have this trait.
3. Growing up did you know or feel different than other Hmong people? Did you feel like you didn't belong or felt discriminated based on how you looked?
    I didn't think my hair color was an issue until I was four. My family sold fabric at the swap meets and I went along to help. Elder Hmong women who came to buy fabric would scold me to not touch anything they planned to buy because I was a *"menyuam pojnxtoog plaubhau daj, qhovmuag xiav"* (blonde-haired blue-eyed demon child). I don't have blue eyes, by the way. My eyes are a lighter shade of brown than most other Hmong people. That was the first time I felt rejected by people of my own ethnic background and realized that my hair color was going to be a trait that people would make into an issue. When I got to my early teens I was often mistaken as a "gangster" because it was trendy for rebellious Hmong girls to bleach or highlight their hair to lighter colors so I often got the stink eye without doing anything.

4. Have you ever competed in a Mr. or Miss Hmong Pageant? If you haven't, did you ever consider doing one?

   No, I never competed in a Miss Hmong Pageant. My family owns a business and we were regularly asked to sponsor the contestants so competing would have been bad for business and since the community is very closely knitted, many people would assume unfair judging if I was to win, which will also lead to bad business and the end of many relationships.

5. Have you thought about competing in a Mr. or Miss Hmong Pageant but decided not to due to your phenotype?

   No. I cried for a whole afternoon about being hated and judged due to my hair color when I was four. I also decided after that long cry, when I was four, that I was above all the judgment and hatred, so I never let any of that judgment bother me anymore.

6. Would it be okay for me to contact you to follow up on these questions?

   Of course.

7. Any other thoughts/stories/comments/questions?

   No, most people think it's pretty amazing.

   Thank you!

Figure 8. Hmong Phenotype Study Survey; Gloria Lee

Name: Sauci Xiong
Age: Twenty-two
Gender: Female

Hmong Phenotype Study

1. How do you identify yourself?
   As a twenty-first century American Hmong girl living in California, post-Vietnam war.

2. How many other Hmong people do you know that exhibit the same or similar phenotype (lighter/blonde hair color) like you? Anyone else within your family?
   fifteen other friends and family members.

3. Growing up did you know or feel different than other Hmong people? Did you feel like you didn't belong or felt discriminated based on how you looked?
   I never felt discriminated in fact felt more like I fit in since I grew up in a heavily populated Caucasian area. I knew I was different but it didn't bother me. I used to Hmong dance. One year, my sister and I (she has yellow hair too) had to die our hair to "match" the other girls. I didn't like the idea. By the date we were supposed to perform, it faded back to yellow. I haven't dyed my hair since then. My hair is a part of me and is what makes me unique.

4. Have you ever competed in a Mr. or Miss Hmong Pageant? If you haven't, did you ever consider doing one?
   I have done multiple Hmong and American pageants. For Hmong: Little Miss Hmong, Miss Hmong Merced, Miss Waterfest, Miss Hmong California, Miss Hmong International. I loved doing them. It was so much fun for my family and I. Going into pageants, all other contestants felt they had an advantage over me because they have black hair which is favored in Hmong pageants as being the idealistic Asian beauty. My mom has told me to dye my hair black multiple times for pageants. I always decline.

5. Have you thought about competing in a Mr. or Miss Hmong Pageant but decided not to due to your phenotype?

No.

6. Would it be okay for me to contact you to follow up on these questions?

Sure. Email or FB is preferred.

7. Any other thoughts/stories/comments/questions?

Let me know what conclusion you come to at the end of your research.

Thank you!

Figure 9. Hmong Phenotype Study Survey; Sauci Xiong

Name: Jimmy Fang
Age: Twenty-three
Gender: Male

Hmong Phenotype Study

1. How do you identify yourself? Hmong American
2. How many other Hmong people do you know that exhibit the same or similar phenotype (lighter/blonde hair color) like you? Anyone else within your family? I know very few people who have it outside of my family including my immediate and extended family. From a family pedigree I compiled with my roommate, it's clear that the phenotype is paternally silenced but maternally expressed. My mom used to have the hair color when she was younger but it faded as she reached puberty.
3. Growing up did you know or feel different than other Hmong people? Did you feel like you didn't belong or felt discriminated based on how you looked? I think for the longest time, it never occurred to me that I was different until I was around five when I started to go to school. There it became clear that I looked different than other Hmong people and as I went through the K-12 system, it was obvious that I was the only Hmong person who looked the way I did. A part of me never really fit in with the other Hmong kids growing up and I came to believe it was because of my hair color. I knew this especially when I went out with my family to the grocery store or restaurant, people would talk about me under their breaths. When I do hear it, it usually goes into questions about whether I'm adopted, whether I'm mixed, whether I dyed my hair, and whether I'm Hmong.

4. Have you ever competed in a Mr. or Miss Hmong Pageant? If you haven't, did you ever consider doing one? Yes, I competed in the 2009 Mr. Hmong Pageant that was organized by CSU Fresno's Hmong Student Union (HMSA). This was their first time putting on such an event and probably was the first of its kind to ever appear on the West Coast. Going into this competition, I thought I had a clear vision of what it was trying to accomplish, promoting higher education via college educated male role models for the community; but, as the weeks approached and the event ensued, it became clear that the beauty pageant became a beauty pageant in the end. Out of all the contestants, I was the only one who had the recessive phenotype. Essentially the pageant broke down to pure aesthetics, where we, the contestants, were being judged based on how we walk down a catwalk wearing casual clothes, formal clothes and our traditional Hmong clothes. During the times where we would answer questions, it was unclear if we were to answer in Hmong or English but I chose to interchange between the two or "Hmonglish." It was tough because a part of me felt during the whole time, I was trying to prove my "Hmongness" to the judges who at that time was a former Ms. Hmong beauty pageant winner, a Hmong rap artist, and a Hmong college counselor.
5. Have you thought about competing in a Mr. or Miss Hmong Pageant but decided not to due to your phenotype? After my experience in the 2009 Mr. Hmong Pageant, I told myself that I would never ever participate in one again.
6. Would it be okay for me to contact you to follow up on these questions? Yes
7. Any other thoughts/stories/comments/questions? I usually always introduce myself with, "This is my natural hair color and I'm 100 percent Hmong." I love getting questions about whether my hair is natural or if it's dyed. Most of the time, people love my hair color and think it's pretty awesome.

Thank you!

Figure 10. Hmong Phenotype Study Survey; Jimmy Fang

Part III: Personal Reflections on Mixed Race

Versions of Myself

James Ong

Being multiracial has always made me feel like an insider *and* an outsider. Everyone around me always seemed to know who they were supposed to be. I identify myself as a multiethnic Asian American—but it's not that simple. I am reminded on an almost daily basis that identity is defined through complex social negotiations. Others constantly define me by "what I am," "what I am not" and "what I *might* be" based on notions of authenticity. The monoethnic rules of identity formation are vexing, exhausting and often contradictory.

This scenario has occurred multiple times and serves as my rubric. If I were to walk into a room of "Asians" and define myself as Chinese, most would accept me but with caveats. If I were to walk into a room of Caucasians and claim my cultural whiteness, I would almost certainly be denied. So what am I?

Engaging with these difficult conversations can be painful, but disengaging means surrendering my ability to define myself. Existing at the intersection of multiple cultures, racial histories and ethnic identities has been both challenging and empowering. My lived experiences as an *in-between being* are ultimately empowering and have given me a critical perspective of the world.

My father is a second generation Chinese American born to pre-Cold War Toisanese immigrants. His parents spoke a distinct dialect from a very specific region of the Pearl River Delta, the same home village as thousands of other early Chinese immigrants to the United States. My grandfather was a *paper son*; my grandmother had to wait for the Magnuson Act of 1943 to come to the United States. The Ongs settled in a Black neighborhood. Dad's exposure to Chinese culture outside of their home was limited. As the first son, others expected him to uphold traditional values. Like many children of immigrants, he eventually Americanized. Though proud of his heritage, he hasn't spoken Chinese in over forty years. My father raised me to believe I was Chinese, yet his efforts to impress this culture upon my brother and me were more or less symbolic.

My mother is from a long-established Germanic American family. She lived abroad in Germany for several years. German foods, cultural knickknacks and nursery rhymes were common in our home. This cultural identity was so influential I seldom acknowledged my mostly absent Italian heritage. Moreover, it dovetailed seamlessly with most mainstream American cultural values.

Their divorce meant exposure to two distinct cultural worlds and growing up in predominately white lower-middle class Bay Area suburbs that severely lacked diversity. I knew my identity was complicated from a very young age. More than anything, I was simply unable to comprehend or provide a persuasive answer to the "what are you" question. My twin brother and I had no other Asian American friends. *Passing* was out of the question; I looked "Asian enough" to be labeled as such. Peers targeted me with "harmless" Orientalist jokes that made me feel like a complete outsider. My first grade teacher convinced the class I was Buddhist because of my last name.

Adolescence only exacerbated my confusion. Racist jokes became more frequent, intentional and acerbic. Out of desperation to fit in, I embodied and even perpetuated these stereotypes. During high school I tried being a cultural chameleon. While acknowledging my Chinese ancestry, I claimed a white cultural identity. This failed spectacularly. At a dinner one night during senior year, without warning, my mother apologized because I was a "half individual in a society that wouldn't accept me as white or Chinese." Realizing the truth in her candid statement was one of the most painful moments of my life.

College was my opportunity to reorient my values and reclaim my surrendered identity. I took East Asian history courses, learned about contemporary Asian American trends, and connected with others with similar cultural perspectives. Rather than lament my Chinese heritage, I embraced it.

Unfortunately, my white suburban sensibilities assumed being "Asian" was a universally meaningful identity. Wrong. Skeptics demanded proof of my authenticity through language skills or cultural knowledge, which of course I had neither. Some Asian American classmates invalidated my heritage because I didn't grow up in an ethnic neighborhood. At the same time, international students emphasized our vast cultural distance by labeling me an ABC (American Born Chinese). Some classmates with no Asian ancestry whatsoever took race completely out of the conversation and claimed their knowledge of East Asian culture made them more Asian than I was.

My first trip to Japan in the summer of 2007 gave me the direction I so desperately craved. Though I spoke zero Japanese and had an extremely limited understanding of the culture, there was an instant resonance with people and spaces. I was enamored by the aesthetics, social mores, diets, designs, and most importantly, the history. I also learned English was a skill in demand.

Japan gave me a sense of purpose and motivation to pursue a career in higher education in a related field. When I returned to UC Santa Cruz in the fall, I immediately changed majors and enrolled in Japanese languages courses. Some commented on how "interesting" it was that a Chinese American wanted to learn Japanese over Mandarin (not Cantonese). I had been raised a mixed Asian American, racialized as such and denied my Chinese heritage; I was going to own my surrendered "Asian" identity despite criticisms. After a crashed economy, several interviews and a very long wait, I finally found a job teaching in Gifu City.

Living in Japan brought more confusion and clarity. My physical appearance perturbed some students and parents. I did not look like their previous foreign teachers yet I was certainly not Japanese. During my first month, a parent boldly approached me and asked, "What are you?" Many of my students were curious about my background. I even had a few mixed students I connected with over the school year. Identity played a clear role in how these students were treated by their peers. When I addressed potential issues with my colleagues, they told me I was imagining things.

Yet, being a mixed Asian in Japan had its advantages. The Japanese adage, "a nail that sticks out gets hammered down" strangely did not apply to my situation. I have no Japanese ancestry, but I felt accepted. Unlike my friends, I was more or less able to blend in, at least until I opened my mouth. People did not approach me as an exotic foreigner; I took the train, shopped and went to ball games without anyone taking notice of my existence. Friends and strangers were genuinely encouraging about my reasons for studying Japanese culture. For once, I at least didn't look and feel like a complete outsider.

It was around this time when I found the field of multiethnic and multiracial studies. Books like *Mixed Blood, The Sum of Our Parts*; *Half and Half*; and *When Half Is Whole* inspired me to engage with these difficult identity conversations on an intellectual level.[3] I connected with various scholars in the field who taught me to value my experiences and critical perspectives. With their encouragement, I applied to graduate school. The UCLA Asian American studies M.A. program helped me develop the skills to articulate my thoughts on the complexity of being a multiethnic Asian American identity. I read hundreds of books, researched, published and taught courses on mixed identity. I found allies and a community of scholars who understood my challenges.

So what does this all mean? Every day is a new opportunity to apply what I have learned for the benefit of others through storytelling and critical analysis. Multiraciality exposes the fiction of race by disrupting presupposed connections between phenotype and cultural affinity at both the interpersonal and structural level. It forces us to acknowledge the inherent plurality of what we consider stable, singular identities. Multiethnic individuals prove that race and ethnicity are fluid concepts, dependent upon individual circumstances, situational interpretations and prevailing social norms.

---

[3] See Williams-León, T. & Nakashima, C. L. (Eds.), (1998). *The sum of our parts: Mixed-heritage Asian Americans*. Philadelphia: Temple University Press, & O'Hearn, C. C. (1998). *Half and half: Writers on growing up biracial and bicultural*. New York: Pantheon Books. See also: Spickard, P. (1989). *Mixed blood: Intermarriage and ethnic identity in twentieth century America*. Madison: University of Wisconsin Press, & Murphy-Shigematsu, S. (2012). *When half is whole: Multiethnic Asian American identities*. Stanford: Stanford University Press.

I have found self-worth in embodying racial dissonance. I accept myself for who I am as someone *in-between*, defined by my Chinese ancestry and family's history, the values I adopted during my time overseas and the racial expectations my Asian American phenotype elicits. There is empowerment in knowing you can choose to be an outsider *and* connected to multiple identities. I am authentically me.

Beautiful As Any Other

Maria Cristal Plantt

Red. Yellow. Blue.
The primary colors that mix into—
orange, violet, and green.
But these are only a few
colors that can create a beautiful art scene.

A painter mixes the colors she needs
and shades them into her canvas
where she frees
her suppressed emotions that everyone sees.

The choice to blend or not to blend colors,
makes her heart flutter.

People often ask why painters decide to mix certain colors,
but her reply is not why, but why not,
if they create such a beautiful piece of art that utters,
I am as beautiful as any other.

Everyone sees my mother's desires
for the man of a different race.
He brings happiness to my mother's face,
but for my grandmother that is not the case.

My grandmother asks my mother why she wants the man
of a different race?
My aunt asks my mother why she desires the man
of a different race?
My mother's friends ask my mother why she wants to have a child
of a mixed race?
Mother replies why not,
if it brings happiness to my face
and is beautiful as any other.

Her heart flutters
because she has the choice to blend with any color.

Caucasian. And Latina.
Two primary races and once mixed—
create a woman of mixed race, me.
But I am only one of many.
We may have been doubted and disregarded,
but now we stand as successful students at UCLA
and are as beautiful as any other

A Mixed Hollywood

Kathryn Loutzenheiser

Mixed Histories Time Traveling

Welcome aboard! I take it you are all informed about the journey that we are about to embark upon. Please fasten your seatbelts and send your last farewell text to your loved ones and let us begin a bit of Mixed Histories Time Traveling through space and place. *The first jump is usually the hardest so try to imagine you're somewhere safe in your beds for a second.* Young Kathryn was born here in the Kaiser Permanente hospital on Sunset/Vermont in East Hollywood in late 1993. Whoosh back a few years and we will see her parents spontaneously getting married in a small chapel in the '80s. *Now make sure to keep a hold on your hat for this one; time traveling can be a bit windy.* Here we see her five-year old mom traveling on a train from El Paso, Texas to Union Station in Downtown Los Angeles in 1959 when her grandpa left her grandma and moved with his kids to Echo Park. Now we'll go back a few notches to where Kathryn's grandpa moved from Ciudad Juárez, Chihuahua to El Paso, Texas in 1949. A little bit earlier, but still within the vicinity, we will run into her dad moving from Canton, Ohio to Hollywood, California sometime in the 1940s. *Now brace your neck for this one; many passengers experience a most painful whiplash accompanied by very poignant nausea with this particular time jump.* Going back several decades we see her tiny, tiny father born on December 30, 1914. If we went back a few more decades on this route, we would end up somewhere in Germany. As you know, I'm from Los Angeles and can't handle the cold so let's just stay here, yes? I hope you have enjoyed today's trip down Kathryn's lineage that is the root of her mixed experiences: the good, the bad, and the *Why does this have to be this way?* Stay tuned for her constant questioning of self, family drama, given and assumed identities, and eventual acceptance of self with scattered showers of regression back to the feeling of being the fraud.

Personal Introduction

This paper will look at the contradictions between the Hollywood that was promoted in the early twentieth century that is still widely popularized in the media today versus the lives and histories of those who have lived and passed through the geographical area of what is considered Hollywood. This will constitute the broader view of Hollywood, and in turn, my personal history. I will reflect on the parallel between the perceptions of Hollywood versus the reality of Hollywood and the perceptions of being mixed race versus the realities of being mixed race. I will also analyze different photographs of Hollywood's current physical landscape. I include references to history that I have learned from classes and books that I believe are relevant and create space for the reader to look into how certain places or words came to be.

It is important to know history if we are to instigate change. It is important to know that inequalities do not just occur spontaneously but are repeatedly perpetuated by those that it favors and privileges. I have heard the arguments that state that multiracial people are living testament to the reality of a post-racial society. This erases the personal stories of multiracial people and the very real differences that exist between their parents and their histories. It makes multiracial people the faces of racial equality while ignoring the current racially charged police brutality and discrimination that exists in places such as our justice system and educational system. Public education does not give us access to the histories that we need to know to understand how systems of oppression operate and how they are proliferated. It seems that it should be obvious that the Los Angeles Unified School District would teach the history of Los Angeles but I was not exposed to this history until attending UCLA. It may have taken longer or I may never have learned these histories if I was not attending this exclusive university and if I had not chosen a major that offers these courses. I am taking the knowledge I have gained from these courses and am applying it to my lived experiences in order to bring to light some of the histories that are often forgotten.

Historical Hollywood

The growth of Los Angeles was largely promoted by *boosters*, wealthy and influential white men in power who strove to make Los Angeles a great city on their terms (McWilliams 1946, 115). The book *Southern California: An Island on the Land* details how these boosters and the people inhabiting Los Angeles at the time essentially shaped and molded Los Angeles into the city it is today through the erasure of its indigenous and Mexican past, systematic oppression and murder of people of color, labor exploitation, advertisement, and the literal molding of the landscape by permanently channeling the Los Angeles River.

McWilliams (1946) also discusses how Los Angeles and Southern California relied heavily upon its image through the distribution of the *Los Angeles Times* newspaper, romanticized images of the Missions on its orange crate boxes, postcards, and various advertising campaigns to bring its audience, white Americans in eastern states, to Southern California. Hollywood and its film industry were very prominent in the historical as well as current advertising of Los Angeles. Images of Los Angeles and Hollywood were essentially sold. These romanticized images were embedded in people's minds as they sought out something that they could never quite grasp when visiting or moving to this contradictory city.

But Hollywood is more than geography: "Hollywood, as Katherine Fullerton Gerould pointed out years ago, exists only as a state of mind, not as a geographical entity" (McWilliams 1946, 330). This is something that I have come to understand as I have continually responded with increasing annoyance to my UCLA peers' reactions when telling them I am from Hollywood. I can tell that they immediately get the idea of Hollywood that has been fed to us through various media outlets. The place that I call home is not a part of their understanding of Hollywood. The community conditions, poverty and cultural diversity of Hollywood, is glossed over by the façade of Hollywood as a place of white wealth and celebrity. I have asked myself how these reactions from friends and strangers at school could potentially on some scale be harmful and I have wondered how my daily life and the daily lives of those who live within the geographical space that is called Hollywood fit into the politics of memory and erasure. Learning more about the history of both Hollywood and Los Angeles has helped me understand that this erasure is purposeful and is not exclusive to Hollywood or to Los Angeles. It is done on various levels to different communities as an act of oppression and is continually spread through stereotypes, media, humor, as well as through the words of our friends and families.

From what I have learned from Carey McWilliams' (1946) book, *Southern California: Island on Land*, there was nothing really inherently special about Hollywood that led it to be what it is today. McWilliams (1946) writes that motion picture producers were actually first located in the area of Echo Park which was then called the Edendale district and may have moved to Hollywood for its varying scenery and available cheap labor but that is the extent of the knowledge for the choice of location (1946, 331). McWilliams also discusses how the film industry built production studios that separated the industry from the community living in Hollywood, which successfully "made possible the world-wide exploitation of the name Hollywood" (1946, 339). This separation is very relevant to what it feels like growing up in Hollywood today. I am very unfamiliar with the Hollywood film industry and the extent of my knowledge about award shows is that they cause extra traffic in Hollywood and make accessing the Red Line train difficult.

One other aspect of Hollywood's history that I would like to exhume is a particular production code of 1934 that "disallowed 'scandalous' subject matter, such as interracial romance, in films" (Montoya, 2008). I found this information from an *Images of America* book called *Filipinos in Hollywood*. Through historical photos, this book chronicles part of the history of Filipinos living in Hollywood and Los Angeles. This code is one of many that worked to segregate communities and curtail interethnic solidarity.

Redlining

Another aspect of Hollywood ripe for viewing via a mixed race lens is historical redlining. Redlining refers to when the Home Owners' Loan Corporation (HOLC, 2014) delineated maps in 1935 to demarcate the security of real estate investment in certain areas. These surveys were basically a way to document where low income and people of color resided.

Certain color codes were used in these maps to reflect the racial covenants that were put into place by white homeowners to prevent people of color from moving into their neighborhoods, particularly targeting Black communities. What one begins to realize when analyzing these maps is that living conditions today are eerily similar to what was documented in the 1930s. These maps show the de facto racist and classist segregation that systematically existed and continues to exist to this day. In reviewing one of these maps of Hollywood, I realized that I grew up within a marked red area with my single mother in a low-income household. In my head there exists a mental map of the more affluent and less affluent areas of Hollywood and what streets act as these markers. When I looked at that map I saw a ghost of the stratified Hollywood I currently know. On the website, one can view the actual surveys that were filled out by the HOLC. This was the prognosis for Hollywood:

> Maintenance is generally of poor quality and population is extremely heterogeneous and includes many subversive racial and social elements. Multiple family structures, of which there are many, are generally of low grade and poor character; some of them located in the lower eastern section are said to be operated on a "bawdy house" basis. Japanese and Filipinos are scattered throughout the area with a concentration of them on streets north of Hollywood Cemetery, which is also an unfavorable influence. Mexicans are located in the blocks adjoining the cemetery on both its east and west borders. The section north of Santa Monica Blvd. and west of Gower St., known as the Colo Estate Tract, is of much better character than the rest of the area, and prices and rentals are materially higher. Were it not for a scattering of Japanese and Filipino residents this section would be entitled to a higher grade. The area as a whole is assigned a "medial red" grade (T-Races, 2014).

It is worth researching these maps and the racist language in the paperwork filled out by the surveyors of these cities.

Me/Me in Hollywood

It has taken me a very, very long time to accept myself as everything that I am rather than trying my best to squash down or change certain aspects of my identity. Different situations may pull one of my identities to the forefront, but I am always all of my identities at once. I am all of my experiences and I am all of my choices. Not only do I identify as multiracial, I am also attracted to all genders (panromantic/biromantic) and am asexual in a sexualized world while also identifying as genderfluid. And I am not at all sorry to be "deviant" in more ways than one.

I am always very conscious of how people view me and how they are categorizing me in their heads when I am in public, especially depending on where I am. I expect most people to see me as exclusively white, cis woman, and heterosexual. I have all the privileges that come with those identities. But those identities aren't the whole of who I am. I often search for ways to bring my mixed identity into a conversation and I always feel myself questioning my right to claim a mixed identity because while growing up I was always told that white was the extent of my racial identity. I always told people I was Mexican and German but the grand sum of it was always white. Even though I grew up with my Mexican-American mother within my mixed Mexican family, that heritage and culture was erased by the fallacy of the supremacy of whiteness in how others defined me. Others also often inflated my German ancestry even though I grew up with no familiarity to German culture. Then I went through a time of trying my best to stamp out anything within myself that fit into a white identity. It has been a poisonous cycle of trying to mold myself into how I want others to see me, when I really don't owe anyone anything.

It is difficult to analyze oneself because we are too close to the subject. But when I do, I tend to lapse into third person. I cannot give an accurate account of the psychological work done on my younger self up to today but I can muse on how the world around me, particularly "Hollywood"/popular media, has influenced my thought processes. Little Kathryn was told she was white and her skin was lighter than her family's and friends. This didn't account much into little Kathryn seeing herself as an outsider and that can be attributed to whiteness being glorified. Some of the times she was told she was beautiful may be attributed to the racism and colorism in the speaker attributing her beauty to her skin color. Kathryn would see the magazines and the movies and the television shows that were saturated with whiteness but she did not see herself in these people. The media probably, most definitely, never taught her to hate the color of her skin or her hair through a larger scale of racial oppression, but she did not feel any connection to the people she saw in the media. She thought she should, and she thought she and everyone else was expected to and will someday live the lives she saw acted out on screen, but that is not what was reflected in her life. Her family and friends did not have excess money; they barely had enough to pay the rent and buy food. They were not the hip young white people living out their twenties in upscale apartments while courting the next door heterosexual love interest. There has always been a barrier between what the media has told us we should have and be and what our realities are. And there has always been a barrier between how others view me and who I really am.

Going Home to Hollywood

The following is a scribbled entry from my journal while I was riding the Line 2 bus from UCLA home. I think it's how I came to write this paper:

June 18, 2014

I think the root of my annoyance and anger at tourists isn't exactly that there are too many or that they crowd up Hollywood Blvd, but rather, just what the hell are you all here for, what did you come here looking for and expecting? This is my home town, it's not a fucking Hollywood movie, this is poverty, this is displacement, these are immigrant communities, this isn't your red carpet high end actress and actor town. They don't fucking live here, they come to show their faces for the camera, block the streets, probably litter and then they get to drive back to their comfortable lives in Beverly Hills and Brentwood. Kindly fuck off with your notions of what my home should be. And when you leave with unmet expectations and feel let down don't say shit about how Hollywood is crap and dirty and that there's too many homeless people. What were you expecting in a town that's known for elite white people? The people who actually live here don't actually matter, do we?

This frustrated journal entry ties in with how the histories and existence of people of color are systematically erased and belittled. Going back to Hollywood to visit has become more interesting and unsettling as I have gotten older and become more aware of structural racism. As I became more self-conscious, I became more aware of the questioning looks that I received when walking around my neighborhood. I moved out in my second year of college so I am not a familiar face to the people who live in my neighborhood. My social anxiety doesn't help with creating amicable familiarity either. I have noticed that it is not common to see someone who looks white walking around in my neighborhood. My self-consciousness, in going home, stems from me being more aware of how others see me and from becoming aware of how I would view myself from an outside perspective.

Geographical Landscape of Hollywood through Photos

Murals depicting famous celebrities, from left to right: Elvis Presley, Arnold Schwarzenegger, Marilyn Monroe, The Beatles.

This is on Santa Monica/Wilton, two blocks from where my mom lives and where I lived during high school and also two miles southeast from the central Hollywood/Highland tourist destination. Viewing the murals while standing on the southwest corner of the street we see a small plaza that houses a small donut shop, a flower shop, a beauty salon, an insurance firm, a Oaxacan panaderia, a Salvadoran restaurant and an electronics shop. I did not use to think much of this until recently when it began to look like a contradiction to me. The famous white singers and actors are a part of the physical landscape and are embedded in what most know as part of the Hollywood entertainment history. From this angle they are juxtaposed and partly blocked by the establishments that currently exist here. This to me appears as a futile attempt of Hollywood to hold on to an image that it took years to carve out and establish. It is still holding on to the memory and fantasy of a glamorous Hollywood.

Hollywood High School's sign that reads, *Free meals for children ages 1-17 M-F 10AM.*

The central Hollywood/Highland tourist spot is one block north of my high school. This sign alludes to the poverty that exists in Hollywood even when so close to the grandeur of the stars on the ground on Hollywood Blvd. and the consumer wonders of the Hollywood Highland Mall.

People selling food on corner of Santa Monica and Western

This is a picture I took in Hollywood while trying to not feel like a tourist. It is on the corner of Santa Monica/Western, a few blocks from where I used to live. There are people selling food on each corner of this cross street. I find this very important because they are physically taking up space in Hollywood with their own economy and are a part of the cultural landscape.

Food workstation on Hollywood Walk of Fame

This is another example of food being sold on sidewalks in Hollywood. This photo shows this workstation set up and claiming physical space on Hollywood Blvd on top of the stars that depict the film industry stars of old. Those stars are a part of the sidewalk from years ago and this cart is a part of the current Hollywood and the lives of the people currently residing in Hollywood.

Conclusion

I thank you all very sincerely for joining me on this Mixed Histories Time Traveling journey. If you will grant me a few more minutes of your time I wish to leave you all with a final parting speech along with your complimentary gift bags. Hollywood is a very mixed span of miles, which is reflected in my high school and in my neighborhood. The reality of what Hollywood is today is rooted in a history that should not be forgotten because it informs the negative and positive aspects of this city's history that are often silenced. On a personal level, going home to Hollywood from Westwood, where UCLA is located, feels like finally escaping from a constricting box. It is where I can go be with the people I care about who are what I mean when I say "home"; where I can eat food that I grew up with that tastes like "home"; where I can hear the language that I grew up around being spoken constantly and more often than English. That is what Hollywood is to me. Not the name, not the industry, but everything that I call home as well as the whispers of the histories lived in this geographic area that I hope can be strengthened into shouts of empowerment for the communities surviving in this city. My mixed self traverses this city and will continue to learn the histories that have been forgotten and will fight to bring them to the foreground of our consciousness.

Bibliography

McWilliams, Carey. *Southern California: An Island on the Land*. New York: Duell, Sloan & Pearce, 1946.

Montoya, C. M. *Filipinos in Hollywood*. Charleston, SC: Arcadia Publishing, 2008.

Pangean

Sophia Cole

Hafu, half blood, half-caste, chimera, mulatto, half breed, and mutt are just a few of the many racial epithets that people have used over the generations to label someone like me. This is problematic because I find that such words have no purpose other than to measure me as less than whole on the racial purity scale. It reminds me of forced sterilization, segregation, anti-miscegenation laws, genocide, scientific racism, and eugenics and many other movements. It reminds me of how such techniques were and are used within the United States of America to suppress, separate, dehumanize and even exterminate groups of people, all in the name of protecting another group's racial purity. Am I angry? Yes, but I feel any decent human being should be angry and sickened by any crime against humanity. On the bright side, my multiracial existence is an indicator of America's failure at keeping racial groups separated. On the other hand, I am stuck in a world where the majority treats me like an anomaly. This is a story about how the social constructions of race have shaped my identity, crafted my environment, and formulated my life experiences.

My name is Sophia Kie Kunito Cole and I was born and raised in Los Angeles California. My parents hoped that I would identify myself with both racial groups. Thus, they gave me two first names. Sophia being my American name and Kie being my Japanese name. I also received both of their last names. Kunito from my mother and Cole from my father. Unfortunately for me, I was not born into a society where having multiple names is considered normal. I was born into a system that expects only one name. One first name, one last name, and almost always one race. So in order for me to function in this society, I often find myself negotiating between my multiracial world and society's monoracial one. My two first names turned into one legal first name, Sophia. As for the "Pick one race" questionnaires that often times appear in official documents, I learned to respond to them depending on the situation. I say I learned how to tackle "pick one race" questionnaires because it took a lot of practice. When I was young, I remember running into the "pick one race" question on standardized tests in Elementary school. I did not understand how such questions could be used to assess student academic achievement by race. All I knew was that this was an important test and that I was to try my best not to make any mistakes. The instructions clearly stated that I had to bubble in one race, but I was more than one race. So I would ask the teacher what to do and every time the teacher was caught completely off guard and did not know how I should answer either. Regardless, I felt like no matter how I answered, I was doing something wrong. If I picked one race I would be lying to the application. If I picked more than one, I would not be following the directions. It wasn't something my parents could teach me either, considering their racial identity was always listed, and they felt equally perplexed when it came to filling out race based applications about me when it stated "check one race." No one seemed to have the answer, so over time I taught myself how to tackle such questions by my own logic. I would make my decision while screaming in my head, "Why do you have to do this to me? I am Black AND Japanese, not Black OR Japanese? What do you expect me to do? Apply the one drop rule to myself? I am very comfortable with who I am. I am not confused by my multiracial identity. The world is the one that is confused and I wish the world would stop making it my problem." Unfortunately no matter how hard I tried, I found it impossible to escape the racial politics that I was born into or to prevent the social constructions of race from impacting my life.

I wish I could say that my African American identity was created through self-identification but it wasn't. It was crafted with the guidance of generations of racist social and political elements. I identity as African American because my father identifies himself as African American. My father is African American because his parents are African American. His parents (my grandparents) are African American because the law said so. My grandparents were born in the South during the time when the

"One Drop" rule was applied. They identify themselves or were forcibly identified as African American/Black/ or Negro even though they have Native American, Irish, and other European ancestors. In a way, this is how the Unites States' racial past manifests itself into the future. Due to laws that shaped my grandparents identity, my identity is African American and Japanese, instead of African American, Japanese, white, and Native American.

I was born and raised in South Central Los Angeles and it wasn't really by accident, either, because the social constructions of race have crafted my environment. Due to my grandparents being labeled as Black, they were treated as such and therefore were prevented from living anywhere they wanted to. Banks, real estate agents, federal agencies and other race-based home loaning practices became agents of segregation by supporting redlining and housing discrimination. Like many other African Americans, the color of my grandparents' skin became the only variable as to why they settled in South Central Los Angeles when they moved from the South. It was a combination of lack of opportunities along with safety in numbers against whites who opposed racial integration. So, regardless of whether or not they had the means to move to a place like Beverly Hills, they were not allowed to move to Beverly Hills due to the color of their skin. Even if they were to successfully move in, the white neighbors and the Beverly Hills police would have made it clear that they were not welcome. Unfortunately, this sort of anti-Black behavior still exists in 2015 launching the #BlackLivesMatter movement. It is really sad how blackness is treated like a sickness in this country and how some people react to the problem by pretending the problem does not exist or that it is a thing of the past. My father was also forced to endure similar lack of opportunities due to the color of his skin, which is why my family ended up living in the same neighborhood as my grandparents. As a result, segregation and racial discrimination would contribute to the fact that I was born and raised in one of the many ethnic enclaves throughout Los Angeles. In Los Angeles, places like Beverly Hills, Westwood, and Bel Air are known as white people neighborhoods, while Compton, Watts, and South Central LA are all code for Black neighborhoods. Koreans have Koreatown and Los Angeles' Japanese population lives in Little Tokyo, Gardena, and Torrance.

The social construction of race mapped my space and I was expected to navigate through it.

I was raised in a predominately African American neighborhood, and because of this I was exposed to my cultural heritage and suffered alongside people who shared my history. My father was very adamant about exposing me to positive aspects of the African American identity and shielding me from all negative ones. When the LA Riots occurred, we never talked about how or what the beating of Rodney King and the shooting of Latasha Harlins should have meant to me or what it meant to the African American community. We never talked about the negative portrayal of blackness or racism against Blacks. But with shovels and brooms in hand, we did go out and help sweep up the supermarket and other stores down the street that were burned during the riots. One could say my father provided me with a filtered childhood experience specifically shaped to gear me towards a positive and balanced identity of being African American and Japanese. Given the fact that we lived in a rough neighborhood where my dog was shot by a drug dealer, who was later arrested for raping a neighbor, I would have to say my dad did his best to filter my experience for my protection. However, he couldn't protect me from everything and, like everyone else, I had to suffer the negative stigma attached to living in what some people refer to as the "ghetto." I had to endure negative stereotypes applied to Blacks. I also had to overcome the racial inequalities that were passed down to the African American youth, such as having unequal access to a good education.

Growing up in an African American ethnic enclave of South Central LA during the 1980s and 1990s greatly shaped my identity as an African American woman, but at the same time it cruelly showed me how I could stand with them but will never be accepted as one of them. Due to preconditioned notions of blackness that were created before I was born, I would never be fully accepted as an African American because I did not fit society's expectations of what an African American looks like. It seemed like people already had an idea of what a Black person is and my face was not one of them. I noticed that there was a difference between how the community interacted with my father and how they interacted with me. As I grew older, I noticed that without my father, my right to be part of the African American Community was often compromised.

Although I am emotionally invested and equally impacted by African American history, other African Americans would rarely accept me as one of them. At school, there would be support groups geared towards African Americans such as African Student Unions. Often times when I go to African American communities, I am stared at and treated as an "outsider." During discussions on the Black experience, often times someone would mention how mixed people don't count towards the Black experience. They say this is because they are not socially treated as Black and therefore wouldn't understand the feeling of being discriminated against due to their phenotypical characteristics. In such situations, I do not bother to respond. Instead, I think about how many times I have been discriminated against by my own people for not being "Black enough." At the same time, I look around at the different people and laugh at the idea of how "African Americanness" is treated as a monoracial category that is pure. Looking at America's racial history and the formation of the Black race, African Americans went through countless classifications. The 1890 census provided the options quadroon, octoroon, and mulatto for biracial Black/white individuals. Then, in the 1920s, multiracial Blacks were categorized as Black (Hochschild and Powell, 2008). Looking at the history of racial categorization in the United States, a large portion of African Americans could be multiracial without even realizing it. However, instead of the African American communities viewing themselves as multiracial, they follow the historically constituted monoracial forms of human classification that were created by the suppressive hegemonic Anglo Americans.

Yet, instead of getting into a heated argument with those who object to me being Black, I try to make my identity more recognizable for those unable to understand that some people are capable of being more than one race and culture. I often ask my dad to come to at least one of the events or I tell them where I was born and raised. Sometimes I try to provide visual cues of my identity by showing them the naturally curly and fluffy state of my hair. If this doesn't work, there are also the verbal cues of being versed in African American vernacular. I do all of this not because I am insecure about my identity, but more to persuade them to treat me as one of them and not an outsider.

I can't help that I look the way I do. I can't change the fact that I was born in a society with preset notions of what a Black person is, and that I don't exactly fit those definitions. So what am I supposed to do? I look questionably Black, just as much as I look questionably Japanese. I refuse to be nothing because I do exist and I do have an identity. So what am I? I am Black and Japanese. I am Western and Eastern. My ancestors built America and I am first generation American because my mother is from Japan.

My mother is Shin-Issei Japanese from Kyoto, which has a history of over 1200 years. She came to the United States in 1988, long after World War II. I also feel it is important for me to dissolve any assumptions and stigmas attached to marriages between Americans and the Japanese, especially since the man who issued my United States passport couldn't even resist such assumptions. No, I am not a war baby love child, and no my father is not in the military, and no my mother is not a picture bride. My Black father is always around and my parents are in their twenty-eighth year of marriage.

However my father's interaction and interest in Japan was not completely detached from militarism. My African American grandfather fought in World War II and was stationed in Japan. My African American grandmother went to Japan to be with her husband. Then in Japan, my father was conceived but was born in the United States. So in a sense, my dad's interest in Japan branched off from political and social events that occurred before he was born. His father was in the military and he was made in Japan.

Los Angeles's geography helped me to form a cultural connection with Japan. I grew up in a predominately African American neighborhood, but Japanese enclaves such as Little Tokyo and Gardena were only a short car ride away. These places helped me to understand the Japanese culture, and to better understand myself. The neighborhood I grew up in was a huge part of my life, but only represented a part of me, and Little Tokyo helped me unlock the rest.

When I was young my mother had me attend the Gardena Buddhist Church, where she worked. I learned Japanese and a little bit about Buddhism there. I also went to Little Tokyo, which served as a community center for Japanese immigrants like my mother and for other children like me. My parents were very involved with the Little Tokyo community, which contributed to my sense of what Japanese is.

I attended many events and festivals in Little Tokyo. When I was young my parents had me participate in a ceremonial dance called the *Kibimai*. The dance would always be performed in front of crowds of over one hundred people. So I had to look my best. The preparation for the dance was always longer than the routine itself, which gave me plenty of time to look at myself in the mirror. My mother would dress me in a *mikoshouzoku*. White colored creams and powders were applied to my skin, to give a porcelain-white-glow. I would sit in my chair and stare into the mirror for hours and smile at the perfect ghostly white powdered face smiling back at me, while my mom painted red lips over the white powder. This all changed the day a Japanese girl's white painted face invaded my mirror. I looked at her face and then looked at mine and watched as my white porcelain skin turned gray compared to hers. I asked my mom to apply more white makeup and eventually began to do it myself trying to turn my gray skin back to the ghostly white skin I once saw. But no matter how many layers I applied, the Black in my blood seeped through turning me gray again. I did not bother asking my mom why I looked the way I did for I already knew why; instead I made the comment "Mom, I look gray. I can't go out and dance like this." My mom responded, "*Shikata ga nai deshou!*" or, "I don't know what you are talking about, but you look great!" At that point, I was not sure if it was me being self-conscious about my multiracial identity or if my mother really didn't see the difference. The dance went on and in the end I felt I was praised in Japanese just as much as my Japanese American partner was. I guess I performed as well as the monoracial Japanese American and used culture to compensate for the lack of phenotypical Japanese characteristics. Yet when I visited my grandparents in Japan, we had to quietly sneak in so that their neighbors would not see the product of their daughter's dishonor.

My race seems to change depending on the space I am in. But what I find strange is how I am constantly being compared to monoracials. If my multiracial race is to be compared to monoracials of course I will come off as a deficit. I will always be considered as not Black or Japanese enough when compared to those approved by society as Black or Japanese. Of course I will stand out in neighborhoods that are socially constructed and organized by race. Those deemed Black are in the Black neighborhoods like South Central, and those deemed Japanese are in Japanese neighborhoods like Little Tokyo. If race becomes the prerequisite of belonging in a neighborhood, to a history, or to a club, then where am I supposed to go? How am I to be categorized? I will never fit in an African American neighborhood, be represented in Japanese history, or be accepted in an African Student Union. I will always be viewed as meeting only half the prerequisites; therefore I will never be allowed full membership. I feel as if I will always end up as the side dish to the central "monoracial pure race." I find it exhausting to constantly be viewed through the monoracial lens, to be filtered by the monoracial lens, and to be constantly measured by monoracial standards.

At one point in my life I thought there wasn't really such a thing as Black and Japanese history. I thought the union between my parents was an oddity. That was until I decided to do research on Black and Japanese interracially shared spaces within Los Angeles as a class project. That is when I became aware of Bronzeville. Little Tokyo, which is known as a Japanese ethnic community at one point, wasn't. When the people of Japanese descent were sent to Internment camps due to Executive order 9066, a large portion of African Americans moved into Little Tokyo and the area became known as Bronzeville. When the Japanese Americans came back there were no racial riots but instead cooperation between the African Americans and Japanese Americans, as they cohabitated and lived as a multiracial community. For example, The Pilgrim house in Bronzeville served as a recreational center to the African Americans in the community. When the Japanese Americans returned there were no major riots due to labor or housing disputes. Instead, the Pilgrim House formed the Common Ground Committee, to promote a positive atmosphere for racial interactions between African Americans, Japanese Americans, and Latino Americans, turning the Pilgrim House into a shared space and helping to defuse racial tensions (Leonard 2000, 202). Later it was voted without a challenge that the building should be returned because they agreed that the building belonged to the Japanese. Yet when I visited Little Tokyo in 2014, in hopes of finding information on Bronzeville, I found very little that was free and open to the public. The Little Tokyo Visitor Center, the Japanese American national history museum's bookstore, and the Little Tokyo Library did not have any information on Bronzeville. I guess someone decided that transracially shared history was not worth remembering. This made me very critical of history and became my personal reminder of how the mainstream narration of history has been filtered through a monoracial lens and divided by racial categories.

It really is too bad that I can't single handedly change the social construction of race. Sometimes, I wish that I could wake up in the morning and think I am Black and Japanese and then suddenly the whole world would adjust and accept my multiracial identity. No more "pick one race" or "pick one name." I wish the world would stop excluding me for not being Black enough, for not being Japanese enough, or for being mixed race.

In conclusion, racial definitions can be psychologically comforting, confining or liberating but like a Bonsai tree, no matter how beautifully shaped, they are always truncating in potential. Though most people and institutions are still locked in these psychological and social constructs, often using them in limiting and oppressive ways, I strive to transcend these artificial constructs, illusory barriers and impositions. I enjoy the best of both worlds but most importantly strive to maximize my potential as a human being. It is a new world, and I and others like me are on vanguard. I also have my very own word *Pangean* that I created to reflect the recombining of people before boundaries were created and recreated to separate them. I am Pangean and my parents are Pangean. My identity formation consisted of a lot of external factors that were completely out of my control. Before I was even born, the social constructions of race shaped my identity, crafted my environment, and formulated my life experiences.

Bibliography

Hochschild, Jennifer L., and Brenna M. Powell. "Racial Reorganization and the United States Census 1850–1930: Mulattoes, Half-Breeds, Mixed Parentage, Hindoos, and the Mexican Race." *Studies in American Political Development* 22, no. 1 (Spring 2008): 59-96.

Leonard, Kevin A. "Brothers Under the Skin? African Americans, Mexican Americans, and World War II in California." In *The Way We Really Were: The Golden State in the Second Great War*, edited by R. W. Lotchin. IL: University of Illinois Press, 2000.

The Whole Neighborhood: The Story of One Contemporary Multiracial American Family

Molly Montgomery

Chinese, Irish, German, and Scottish, with a pinch of French. That's how my parents described my ethnic background to me when I was a kid. I knew from the time I was little that I was a mixture of a whole bunch of things, but when it came time to fill in a bubble on the standardized tests that I took in elementary school, I could only choose one race. I usually bubbled in "Other."

On many records, mixed race people are not recognized, or are forced to choose only one race or ethnic identity on paper. Growing up mixed race, I rarely felt torn between choosing one of my ethnic backgrounds over another. Instead of grappling with my racial identity, I was comfortable and proud of my mixed heritage. I found it strange that a whole segment of the population that is like me would be ignored or erased on official forms such as the United States Census until 2000, especially since the multiracial population is one of the fastest growing groups in the United States. The number of people who identified as more than one race on the U.S. Census increased by 32 percent between 2000 and 2010 (U.S. Census Bureau, 2012). Although mixed race people are more visible now than they were before, they have had a long presence in America. In my own experience, I grew up surrounded by people of multiple races and different identities, many of whom were part of my own family.

My family is multiracial, multicultural, and multidimensional, but I never realized it until I went to high school. I didn't notice that some of my cousins were part Asian or part Black or white. I didn't think of my family in racial terms. Nor did I blink an eye at my cousin Patrick who had Down syndrome or my uncle Jim who was born with a genetic condition that gave him only one finger on each hand. That's just the way they were, and it never occurred to me that the world outside might treat my family members differently. Of course, that was a naïve perspective, but as a sheltered child growing up privileged and middle class in urban America, I didn't know what struggles my family members might have faced, nor did I realize just how unique my family really was.

While taking classes at my Catholic high school, I became more aware of issues of institutionalized racism and social justice. I began to view my family from a different light and began to notice that my family was like no one else's that I knew. I grew up in the San Francisco Bay Area, where there is a significant amount of racial diversity and many mixed families. I then attended college at UCLA, where it is also common to meet people who come from a multiracial or multiethnic background. Still, to this day, it is rare for me to meet anyone with a family that can match mine in terms of diversity.

One time, before I was born, my parents took my cousins to the circus. The man taking their tickets remarked, "It looks like you brought the whole neighborhood," seeing their different skin colors, hair colors, and faces. My parents, themselves an interracial couple, politely smiled and told him that, in fact, these children were all part of their family. My mother is Chinese American and my father is white. On my father's side, we have nearly every race in our mix, not to mention I have several family members who identify as LGBT. While most other mixed race families I personally know of have one interracial union while the rest of the family on both sides is monoracial, three of my paternal grandmother's five adult children (including my father) married someone of a different race. As my uncle Jim puts it, "we hit a critical mass of diversity" in my family" (J. Montgomery, in discussion with the author, July 24, 2014).

Discovering this about my family raised several questions for me. Why did such a blossoming of diversity occur in my family in particular? Was it pure chance? Or was there something about my father's family that led to their acceptance of people from different races and cultures? I suspected that there must be more to the equation because my family is more than just diverse on paper. We've always been proud of our inclusion of people of different identities ever since I can remember. But what shaped my family into having such an open outlook? To answer these questions, I looked to the stories of my family members.

My middle class upbringing and my appearance (I take after my dad, who is white) gave me the privilege of not experiencing racism or discrimination personally, but because of that I also grew up unaware of how it had affected my own family. Getting to know my family's stories would not only help me learn about my own heritage, but help me to understand my family members and their struggles better. Along with my family's story, I was searching for something greater--a narrative of how America has grown and changed since the civil rights era, and a clue as to whether we're moving in the right direction. From my investigation, I discovered the story of my family, the Montgomerys. I certainly do not claim that my family's history is representative of most mixed race families. Quite the contrary—mixed race families have a wide range of experiences. However, I do believe that my family's story holds valuable insight into what it means to be a mixed race family in the United States today. My family, especially the couples in my parents' generation, was brought together by greater civic and cultural forces that were shaping California and the nation. But my family stayed together because of something more elusive—a spirit of acceptance and belonging that my family members cultivated across several generations.

My grandfather, Robert Montgomery (January 7, 1929—August 2, 2012) was born with three fingers on one of his hands. His older sister had webbed fingers at birth, so it certainly seemed that there was a genetic component to his disability. My grandfather had *oligodactyly*, which is the state of having fewer than the normal number of fingers and toes. His hand wasn't much of an impediment, in retrospect. It didn't prevent him from attaining an education at the University of California, Berkeley, or becoming an engineer. Today, my grandfather's hand would surprise most people, but after the initial curiosity had worn off, no one would give it a second thought. Unfortunately, when my grandfather was growing up, people were not as open-minded.

My uncle Jim, who inherited my grandfather's oligodactyly, told me that my grandfather (who I call "grandpa Bob") was never comfortable in his own skin due to his disability. Grandpa Bob experienced stares and discrimination throughout his life, which caused him to internalize the idea that he was less of a human being due to his two missing fingers. Once, when he was taken into the hospital for an unrelated health problem, the doctors asked him what was wrong with his hand, and he answered, "I'm deformed." A religious man, my grandfather often remarked late in his life that in heaven, he would have a real hand" (J. Montgomery, in discussion with the author, July 24, 2014).

The worst discrimination that my grandfather suffered was when he proposed to a woman when he was in college. She turned him down at her family's wish. Not because of his economic situation, or his family's status, or because they didn't like him. No, they simply didn't want her to marry someone who had a hand like his. They were afraid that his disability would be genetic, and that it would be passed on to his children. This incident, sadly, was probably one of the most formative experiences in my grandfather's life (B. Gabriel, in discussion with the author, July 20, 2014).

Then my grandmother came along. Betty Montgomery (née Betty Campbell, b. July 15, 1930- d. March 22, 2014) met my grandfather in college, and they were engaged before they graduated. They married on July 7, 1951. Although my grandparents' marriage didn't last— they divorced around twenty years later—my uncle Jim attributes their marriage as the moment when it all began, when the attitude of acceptance that my family has fostered for as long as I can remember came into being (J. Montgomery, in discussion with the author, July 24, 2014). When my grandmother agreed to marry my grandfather, with his three-fingered hand, she set off a chain of events that escalated, eventually, into the inclusive environment of my family today.

In 1976, just nine years after the landmark Supreme Court case *Loving v. Virginia,* which overturned laws banning interracial marriage, my aunt Barbara, a white woman, and my uncle Michael, a Black man, were married in Berkeley, California. Their marriage was the first interracial marriage in my family, and also marked the first marriage of any of my father's siblings. Interracial marriage was not unheard of during this period in California. Anti-miscegenation laws had been struck down much earlier in California, with the California Supreme Court Case's ruling of *Perez v. Sharp* in 1948 (in fact, it was the first ruling to strike down such a law in the United States) (see Loving, 2012). Furthermore, during the 1970s the Bay Area was emerging from a formative period in its history, the civil rights movement.

My grandparents moved to El Cerrito from the rich enclave of Piedmont in the early 1950s. At that time, El Cerrito was a small town. Situated north of Berkeley, it was shaped by the burgeoning civil rights movement activities taking place at UC Berkeley, which were created by students inspired by the movement in the American South. Students at UC Berkeley established a chapter of the Congress on Racial Equality on campus and began to fight for expanded worker's rights for minorities (see Oakland Museum of California, n.d.). California has always had a long history of minority populations, due to the original presence of Native Americans and the Mexican population, and a long-standing population of immigrants from East Asia and other parts of the world, but during the 1940s it expanded due to the migration of African Americans to the West seeking jobs during World War II (see Oakland Museum of California, n.d.). While not all the goals of the civil rights movement were achieved, and racism persists today even in the progressive Bay Area, one of the movement's greatest successes significantly impacted the lives of my father and his siblings: the integration of public schools.

The landmark decision of *Brown vs. Board of Education* in 1954 led to the integration of schools around the country, although it took several decades for it to be fully implemented in California.[4] Many non-white families moved into the neighborhoods during the 1970's, including many Asians. Students from the neighboring Richmond, California, a city with a large African American population, were bussed in to El Cerrito's schools. Due to conservative opposition from white communities, bussing and desegregation took several years to be implemented in the Richmond School District, which included both El Cerrito and Richmond. Nevertheless, by

---

[4] "The 1973 Keyes v. Denver decision established the conditions for getting federal urban desegregation orders outside the South. Keyes required desegregation only when civil rights lawyers proved a violation by showing systematic official action and policies that had the effect of segregating students of color. Therefore, the real impact of Brown did not reach California until the 1970s, and then only through Keyes" (Orfield and Ee, 2014).

1970, when my aunt Barbara was in high school, integration was being phased in to the school district (Rubin 1972).

It was this integration that brought my aunt and uncle together at El Cerrito High School, where they met and began dating. My uncle was bussed in from Richmond, although at the time it didn't strike him as a big deal, because, as he put it, "For me, school stuff was always a hassle, and this was just a little more" (M. Gabriel, in discussion with the author, July 20, 2014).

According to my uncle Michael, during this time period there was a more widespread attitude of appreciation and openness towards non-white minorities in the culture of the Bay Area, due to the momentum of the civil rights movement. Even white Americans, who had before viewed homogenization as the singular goal of successfully integrating into American society, were beginning to reach back to their immigrant roots and identify not as racially white, but as the ethnic mix that most European Americans are (M. Gabriel, in discussion with the author, July 24, 2014). My aunt Barbara to this day views her racial background in terms of her ethnicity— she sees herself as Scottish, Irish, German, and French—not as white (B. Gabriel, in discussion with the author, July 20, 2014).

"Everyone was okay about being different—that was the spirit that was being embraced at the time," my uncle Michael told me. "But it kind of died at some point. I don't know if it's gone away, but it certainly doesn't seem to be as present [today]" (M. Gabriel, in discussion with the author, July 20, 2014). My aunt and uncle went to public high school at a time when children of different races, cultures, and socioeconomic backgrounds were meeting each other and interacting for the first time. My father, who is seven years younger than my aunt, went to El Cerrito High School in the mid-1970s, while at around the same time, my mother, who is Chinese American, attended high school in Alameda, a small town located on an island west of Oakland which was predominantly white at the time. Despite the differences between El Cerrito and Alameda, my parents, my aunt, and my uncle described similar experiences of exposure to friends of other races and cultures. People didn't necessarily group together in cliques by race, my aunt Barbara told me. Instead, social divisions fell more on socioeconomic lines. At El Cerrito high, there were a number of middle class Black students who hung out with their white middle class peers (B. Gabriel, in discussion with the author, July 20, 2014).

At the same time, my father pointed out to me that there was one thing that brought people of all races and classes together: sports. As a football player, my dad often interacted with not just other white students, but also Black and Asian students. His friend group in high school was primarily white and Asian (J. Montgomery, in discussion with the author, July 27, 2014).

My mother's experience, as a person of color in a predominantly white school, was very different from my father's. After attending elementary school and junior high school in a predominantly Black neighborhood where she was often the only Asian kid in the class, my mom moved to Alameda and found herself in an entirely different educational setting. When she was at Alameda High School, there were only two African American students. She wasn't the only Asian student herself, but she was still a part of a small minority of students. My mother told me that she and her friends, who were all different races, were one of the few integrated friend groups at that time, and that people found it kind of "odd" that she, an Asian girl, hung out with a white girl and a Hispanic girl (S. Montgomery, in discussion with the author, July 27, 2014). Perhaps the changes that were being felt so strongly in El Cerrito hadn't yet reached the suburban enclave of Alameda.

At school, my aunt and uncle faced little opposition to their relationship, but unfortunately the open-minded outlook of their generation didn't extend to all of my family. My aunt's maternal grandparents, whom in my family we nicknamed "Mammo" and "Dado" for short, still retained a bigoted attitude towards race. My aunt told me how one time, before she and my uncle were dating, Mammo took her out to lunch in Berkeley. Spotting a Japanese couple at the restaurant, my great-grandmother commented on how it was nice to see that "they were the same." When my aunt married my uncle, Mammo and Daddo acted very strange towards her.

"They were freaked out," my aunt said, and they refused to let my aunt and uncle come to family functions at their house from there on out. On the other hand, the rest of their family, including my grandmother (my aunt's mother), and my uncle Michael's family were entirely accepting of their marriage.

Interracial marriage was no stranger to my uncle's family. Many of his family members came from the New Orleans area, where mixed race families had been common for decades, if not centuries. Even my aunt, who is blonde-haired, blue-eyed and very pale-skinned, was once asked by one of my uncle's family members if she was part Black (B. Gabriel, in discussion with the author, July 20, 2014).

My aunt and uncle's marriage set the precedent in my family for the other interracial marriages that would follow. My uncle, Bruce Montgomery, married a Chinese American woman, Sandra Yee, not long after. After having one daughter, they divorced, and he remarried a second Chinese American woman, Kathi Quan, with whom he had two children. By the time my mother and father were married in 1990, no one blinked an eye, according to my uncle Jim.

Apart from my great-grandparent's reaction to my aunt and uncle's marriage, there was no fuss about any of the interracial marriages in my family. They were just that, marriages, and as in any marriage, you incorporate new people into the family who come from a different background your own and adapt to fit their needs.

When my aunt Barbara and uncle Michael had their first son in 1978, their identity as a mixed race family took backseat to another important issue that arose: my cousin Patrick Gabriel was born with Down syndrome. Down syndrome occurs when a baby is born with an extra chromosome, often resulting in physical and developmental traits including low muscle tone, small stature, an upward slant to the eyes, a single deep crease across the center of the palm, and cognitive delays (see NDSS, 2012). The presence and severity of these traits varies from person to person. People with Down syndrome often attend school, work a job, and pursue creative interests, just like anyone else. In recent years, there has been increased awareness and attention to people with Down syndrome, but throughout my cousin's life, people have not always been understanding.

When my aunt was pregnant with my cousin Patrick, tests for Down syndrome were not common, and so she did not know that Patrick had Down syndrome until he was born. The doctor at the hospital in Oakland, where he was born, pointed out the characteristics to my aunt and uncle, who took the information in stride.

"When Patrick was born I had feeling that . . . it was going to be okay," my aunt told me, "There was just something about him, his person" (B. Gabriel, in discussion with the author, July 20, 2014).

But from the day Patrick was born, he and my aunt and uncle were confronted by peoples' ignorant assumptions about people with Down syndrome. One of the nurses at Kaiser told my aunt after Patrick was born that, "children with Down syndrome are so sweet but they don't live very long." My aunt and uncle immediately set out to confront the prejudices and discrimination my cousin would face from the very start (B. Gabriel, in discussion with the author, July 20, 2014).

Neither my aunt nor my uncle were strangers to disabilities. My aunt had grown up knowing about her father's disability, and she had a younger brother, my uncle Jim, born with one finger on each hand. My uncle's sister had sickle cell anemia, so he was acquainted with disability as well.

"I knew that in life that there are many different kinds of things that happen and people aren't all the same," my aunt said, explaining to me her response to Patrick's Down syndrome. "There were a lot of couples that went into grieving when they found out their child had Down syndrome. And sure, you're somewhat sad that your kid won't have a normal life, but we went more into action" (B. Gabriel, in discussion with the author, July 20, 2014).

In the 1980s, when Patrick was growing up, there was a push to bring students who needed special education back into regular school programs, to give them a more standard school experience where they could develop their full potential. My aunt and uncle advocated to have Patrick educated in the least restrictive setting possible, which is what state law mandates for students with disabilities (see JDC 2016). For Patrick, that meant being in the regular classroom, alongside other children. My uncle joined the planning committees of a new elementary school in Berkeley that was to do exactly that—bring special education students into the same learning environment as regular students.

"We kind of took the more active approach," my uncle said. "We thought, if there isn't a school, make a school. There were a lot of resources for education; we just had to work to seek them out. We really worked hard" (M. Gabriel, in discussion with the author, July 20, 2014). "In any setting, we tried to have Patrick accepted as a person," my aunt told me. She and my uncle to this day still encounter strange and uninformed reactions to Patrick's Down syndrome. She told me that she had experienced one of these moments just this past year, when she was trying to set up a dentist appointment for Patrick through a dentist that accepts DentiCal, the dental insurance plan for people with disabilities. "The receptionist told me they didn't have the equipment to tie him down," she recounted. "I told her he is like any other person. He doesn't need to be tied down."

While I was growing up, I never had any trouble realizing that Patrick was just like "any other person." My earliest memories of him come from playing with him at my grandma's house where he often played at being the Tickle Monster and tried to tickle me. I don't think I was really aware that he had a disability until I was older, in middle school, and even then, it never struck me as important. Patrick was always just Patrick. He's a very distinctive person, as I've discovered in the twenty-two years I've known him. He's obsessed with celebrity gossip, and knows way more about pop culture than I do. He graduated from Oakland Tech High School, and took several art classes. He currently works part-time at a coffee shop near my house and lives at home with my aunt and uncle.

Growing up, I spent a lot of time with my cousins, who are all older than me, at my grandma's house in El Cerrito. We used to have sleepovers with all of us taking over the various rooms that used to belong to our parents when they were growing up. We would watch Disney movies together and eat at Sizzler's for dinner. My exposure to my cousins prepared me for socializing with other kids. I grew up from a young age with a strong sense of community, of belonging. Perhaps this isn't so rare, but I must credit my grandmother for creating an environment where differences between my cousins and I did not become divisive.

At my grandmother's memorial this past April, my cousin Christian Gabriel, Patrick's brother, who identifies as mixed race and gay, gave a speech about how important my grandmother's attitude of unconditional acceptance was to him. His words really struck me as appropriate for summing up her influence on my family:

> At some point my grandmother discovered the revelatory truth that so many people still to this day have yet to realize: that we are all created exactly as we are supposed to be and that love, acceptance and compassion are all

that matters. This was the overarching message her presence taught me as I grew up in our strange, eclectic, multicultural, socially and physically diverse clan (C. Gabriel, Betty Montgomery's Memorial Service, April 26, 2014).

However, there was a dark side to my grandmother's parenting, which affected my dad and his siblings. My grandmother was an alcoholic, and her addiction caused her to be absent from much of her children's lives while they were growing up. When she and my grandfather divorced in the 1970s, she was still mired in her addiction and was not providing as much support for her two children who remained at home: my dad and my uncle Jim. Only in 1982 did she sober up, and she remained sober for the rest of her life, until she passed away in 2014.

During much of his childhood, my uncle Jim had to look to role models other than his parents for support. My grandfather always felt guilty for passing on his condition, and as a result he and my uncle were not close. My uncle also identifies as gay, which my grandfather had a hard time coming to terms with over the years.

My uncle didn't let his disability stand in the way of doing anything. He wears metal prosthetics to aid him, and has no trouble driving a car. He also runs an urban farm in Berkeley with vegetables, fruits, chickens, rabbits, and goats. Growing up, his siblings did not treat him any different. He was the youngest kid, and was picked on just as much as any other baby brother in the family. "When my siblings picked fights with me, they just took into the account that I had the advantage of metal prosthetics," he told me, dryly (J. Montgomery, in discussion with the author, July 24, 2014).

However, during instances when my uncle pointed out he had been treated differently because of his disability, he said that his siblings often dismissed him, telling him that he was making up the discrimination. One of the few people who acted in solidarity with my uncle was a Japanese man named Tom, who moved in with my grandmother after her divorce. Tom and my grandmother were drinking buddies, so he was another enabler of her addiction. Nevertheless, he had a positive impact on my uncle, who considers him a "step-father figure." Tom was sent to an internment camp as a boy during World War II. During the war, his family lost all of the farmland they owned. He was bitter about this for a long time, and thus could relate to my uncle and his struggles with discrimination. My uncle told me that Tom stuck up for him when he faced people staring at him in public.

My uncle, unlike my grandfather, never let people's perceptions of his disability lessen his own self-assurance. In fact, he was very in-tune with his own identity from a young age. At fifteen, he came out as gay to my family, telling everyone except for my grandfather. He became an activist for gay rights in high school, bringing another boy to his prom. While my grandfather was never fully accepting of his son's sexuality, my grandmother and the rest of my family took it in stride. My uncle's activism and simple refusal to be anything that he was not further opened the doors of my family to different identities.

When my cousin Christian was born in 1982, my aunt Barbara said she again had an intuition that Christian was going to be different. My family was no stranger to difference by that point. My aunt and uncle raised their son with an awareness of his mixed heritage, explaining his background to him in terms of ethnicity, not race, as my parents did for me.

Having my uncle Jim in the family helped my uncle Michael be more understanding when Christian came out as gay, he told me. "Having a gay person in the family led to information and education, concerns and fears, during a time when AIDS was going around," my uncle Michael told me. "When someone introduces you to a whole new thing to think about and to have in your life . . . it isn't something that you want to go away, it's just another element to take into consideration" (M. Gabriel, in discussion with the author, July 20, 2014).

Still my uncle told me he had to reexamine some of his unconscious biases. When Christian was a kid he wanted to play with Barbie Dolls, my uncle told me, but my uncle was reluctant to let him. At the time, he thought he was concerned with Christian becoming too "obsessive" over certain toys, but he admitted, "maybe if he had been obsessed with swords I wouldn't reacted as strongly" (M. Gabriel, in discussion with the author, July 20, 2014).

Growing up, Christian confronted taunts and teasing, and in his adult life has occasionally dealt with homophobic slurs. He hasn't faced much overt discrimination due to his perceived race, but because he looks, in his own words, "racially ambiguous," people often make assumptions and stereotype him based on their perceptions of his race or ethnicity. Christian lived in New York City for ten years, and recently moved back to the Bay Area. In NYC, he was often perceived to be Latino, specifically Puerto Rican. And with assumptions came preconceived notions about his personality, economic background, and behavior. "I usually find myself simply explaining my ethnic background much to the surprise of others because it challenges their preconceived notions," Christian told me (In discussion with the author, August 10, 2014).

Christian takes pride in our family's diversity, much like our grandmother did. People often don't understand or believe him when he tells them he has part-Asian cousins. But instead of begrudging people who have a limited view of racial and ethnic identity, he sees it as an opportunity to open their eyes. He told me:

> One thing I really enjoy doing is telling people how many forms of difference our family contains, from the ethnic and cultural differences to the differently-abled aspect as well. It definitely opens one's eyes to the amount of ignorance out there. It's very hard for people to see outside the little boxes they have compartmentalized everything into, and I particularly enjoy challenging them (C. Gabriel, in discussion with the author, August 10, 2014).

Like my cousin Christian, I've encountered my share of situations in which people have made assumptions about my ethnic background. Since my Chinese heritage is not always apparent to people I meet, I often "pass" as white. This has caused countless misunderstandings, which have been mostly harmless. For example, one time in college when my parents sent me a *lai see*, or a red envelope for Chinese New Year, one of my friends saw it and asked if my mother had mistaken it for a Valentine's Day gift. I then had to explain what it was actually for, and that I am, in fact, part Chinese. Some situations have been more sinister. When I was a baby, my mother would take me in a stroller around our neighborhood in Oakland, which was mostly white at the time.

"People would ask me if I was your nanny," she told me. "And I would say no, I'm the mother. I actually gave birth to her" (S. Gabriel, in discussion with the author, July 27, 2014). Unfortunately, this type of occurrence was common while I was growing up: people stereotyping my mother due to her Asian background and finding it hard to believe that she and I are related. I have been asked a few times if I was adopted, but if people took a few seconds to look past the different skin colors that my mother and I have, they would probably see her traits in me.

My uncle Michael Gabriel, on the other hand, told me that the worst he has encountered due to his multiracial family is stares. But he doesn't blame people for their curiosity: "I think one of the dynamics when you have a multiracial family is that people are trying to figure it out," he said. "You look at the parents and the kids and see what the equation equals. Does the child look like the father or the mother? And I think when you see a mixed race family there's a natural curiosity to figure out who belongs to who" (M. Gabriel, in discussion with the author, July 20, 2014).

For me, the value of growing up in a mixed race family is that I've been able to understand my identity in a way that goes beyond racial terms that simplify and categorize people with different experiences and cultures, placing them into rigid boxes.

For example, when I tell people that my grandparents are Chinese, many of them jump to the conclusion that they were born in China, just as many people when they meet my mother ask her where she is from, assuming that because she is Asian she or her parents must be recent immigrants. These assumptions are far from the reality of my family history. People are often surprised to hear that my Chinese family has been in the U.S. since 1882, when my great-great-grandparents immigrated to Hawaii from China, where they established their own bakery. Their grandson, my grandfather John Jay (March 10, 1923-September 26, 2006), grew up on Oahu, where his parents worked at a pineapple cannery. He went to trade school and became a shipwright.

My maternal grandmother's parents immigrated to the U.S. from China in the early 1900's and started their own laundry business in San Francisco. My grandmother, born Eva Lim (November 2, 1922—), grew up in an orphanage in Oakland because her father could not support her or his other children after her mother eloped and left the family. My grandpa John met my grandma Eva through a friend who was visiting Hawaii. He came to see my grandmother in California, and they became engaged and were married in 1950 (E. Jay, in discussion with the author, July 22, 2014).

What is perhaps even more surprising, than my family's long history in the U.S., is how my family has kept its culture intact despite the pressures of assimilation. That's not to say that I am very in touch with my Chinese heritage. Unfortunately, I am not. My mother, who never learned Cantonese herself, did not pass the language to me, and we do not celebrate many Chinese festivals or holidays. Still, I believe my family has done well despite the obstacles it has faced to maintain Chinese culture so many generations down the line.

When I asked my grandmother, who is now ninety-two years old, whether she considered herself more Chinese or American, she said that she is both. She has spent her entire life in the United States, speaks English and Cantonese, enjoys Cantonese food, and watches American soap operas on television. Maintaining her cultural identity has not been easy for my grandmother, who grew up in an orphanage from when she was a baby until she was sixteen. But somehow my grandparents managed to preserve their culture in the United States.

At the same time, my grandparents were open to my mother having an interracial marriage, and did not pressure her into marrying someone Chinese or raise objections. My mother has a strong independent streak, so perhaps that has something to do with their reaction; they knew she would marry whom she wanted regardless of their opinions. The generation prior to my grandparents, much like my great-grandparents on my father's side of the family, would not have approved of marrying outside the Chinese community, my grandmother told me. My grandfather John Jay's mother looked down on her other son Wally's marriage to a woman who was mixed, my great-aunt Bernice. Bernice, born Bernice Kenolaina Tenn, is part-Native Hawaiian and part-German and when she married my great-uncle, my great-grandmother refused to give her jewelry, the traditional gift passed from mother to daughter-in-law in my family's culture. My grandparents, on the other hand, accepted my dad into their family, and embraced me, their only grandchild, wholeheartedly (E. Jay, in discussion with the author, July 22, 2014).

My mother was concerned that I would lose touch with my Chinese identity, so she made sure to expose me to Chinese culture (S. Montgomery, in discussion with the author, July 27, 2014). When I was growing up, my parents and my mother's parents would have dinner every week with me at King Wah, a Cantonese restaurant in Oakland Chinatown that is now closed. My maternal grandparents taught me bits and pieces here and there about their language and culture. Then, when I was seven, my mother started to send me to a Chinese cultural summer program in Oakland called Hip Wah.

Hip Wah, which is a four-week summer program focused on learning Chinese culture and engaging in activities such as brush painting, Kung Fu, and learning to play Chinese musical instruments, became an integral part of my summer breaks. I attended Hip Wah for eight summers. Hip Wah was an eye-opening experience for me, not just because I learned about ancient Chinese history or read the tales of the Monkey King, but also because it was the first time I felt truly felt like I stood out because of how I looked. For the most part, everyone at Hip Wah was fully Chinese, and suddenly, I was the white girl, the one who was asked, "Why are you here?" There were actually a few White children at Hip Wah who had no ethnic Chinese heritage, whose parents had sent them to the camp because they wanted them to learn about a different culture. Although I might have raised a few eyebrows at the camp, I felt like I belonged. After all, I spent summer after summer there with the same friends. And when people met my mother, who served as treasurer for the program, they immediately understood my connection to Chinese culture.

The life and family I have described in this essay might appear to be idealized or overly romanticized. If that is the case, it is because I have been extremely blessed to grow up in the inclusive environment of my family and of California. At the same time, I do not want to overlook the struggles that my family members have faced in the post-civil rights era in the United States. After the civil rights movement occurred in the 1950s and 1960s, there was a hopeful outlook, especially in liberal-minded places like California, that we would soon enter a new stage of history where racial difference would no longer matter. For many of my family members, including my aunt Barbara and uncle Michael, and my parents, this dream of an integrated society became closer to reality because they attended integrated high schools and had friends of many different races. Within my family, whatever discrimination or prejudices my family members would face in the world outside were banished by my family's loving atmosphere, which was cultivated by my grandmother Betty, our family's matriarch.

But, in retrospect, my family's protective bubble also had some downsides. I grew up under the impression that the post-racial vision of America was a reality, when it was not. Thus, when I first encountered discussions of institutionalized racism in my social justice class in high school, I was surprised, more surprised than I should have been. While I am proud of my family's history of treating family members equally no matter their race, disability, or sexuality, I know that this is not how many of my own family members are treated outside of our family gatherings. My uncle Michael is stopped by the police more often because he is Black (M. Gabriel, in discussion with the author, July 20, 2014). My mother has experienced stereotyping, and, on occasion, racial slurs. My Chinese grandparents were barred from buying houses in certain neighborhoods during the 1950s because of their race (E. Jay, in discussion with the author, July 22, 2014). And these are just a few examples—they certainly don't attest to the full breadth of discrimination that people in my own family have felt in their personal life. While I believe that growing up learning that I was a mixture of different ethnicities—Chinese, Irish, German, Scottish—was helpful to me in forming my personal identity, the unfortunate reality in this world is that you will be treated based on how people perceive your race.

The post-racial America where everyone is colorblind to race will not be achieved any time soon, nor is it a realistic hope. School segregation, which was being actively combated through integration during my parents' generation, is still persistent. According to a study by the Civil Rights Project at UCLA, "80 percent of Latino students and 74 percent of Black students attend majority nonwhite schools (50-100 percent minority), and 43 percent of Latinos and 38 percent of Blacks attend intensely segregated schools (those with only 0-10 percent of white students) across the nation," which is not much of an improvement from segregation levels in the late 1960s (Orfield, Kuscera and Siegel Hawley, 2012). According to another study by the Civil Rights Project conducted this past year, "Brown at 60: Great Progress, a Long Retreat and an Uncertain Future," segregation in the South has reverted back to 1967 levels (Orfield, Frankenberg, Ee and Kuscera, 2012).

Being able to interact with people of different races in an educational setting was key to my family members becoming more open-minded and accepting towards people of different races, and led to several of them eventually marrying outside their race. Integration of schools is a social justice issue for minority students in impoverished schools, of course. But I also think another important element of integration is that it fosters compassion and understanding between people of different races and cultures. In fact, the "Brown at 60" report by UCLA asserts, "Integrated schools are linked to reduction in students' willingness to accept stereotypes. Students attending integrated schools also report a heightened ability to communicate and make friends across racial lines (Orfield, Frankenberg, Ee and Kuscera, 2012).

I do not find these conclusions surprising because they correspond to my experience growing up in a multiracial family. I understand the oppression and discrimination people of different races face because I've learned about them from family members or friends that I know personally. That isn't to say being married to someone of another race or being friends with someone of another race absolves you of racism. Far from it, but one would hope it would lead you to rethink any unconscious assumptions you make about people who are different from you.

In my opinion, many of the problems of racism in our world today are exacerbated by a lack of compassion. Reading about unarmed Black children being gunned down, to refugee children being refused safe haven, all too often in the media one hears the perspective of bigoted people who have trouble viewing others who are different from themselves as equally human. I would hope that people would be able to view others with compassion no matter if they're related to someone of that race or if they know someone who shares a particular disability or difference. But if that is not happening spontaneously, we need to bring people of different races together, ask them to listen to each other, and hope that a deeper understanding of their shared humanity emerges. In my own family and in my own life I've experienced the convergence of different races, cultures, and identities firsthand and seen the outcome. While my family isn't perfect, I'm very proud of what we have achieved and hope that the legacy of acceptance and love my family has created reverberates on through future generations.

Bibliography

"2010 Census Shows Multiple-Race Population Grew Faster Than Single-Race Population." U.S. Census Bureau: 2012. https://www.census.gov/newsroom/releases/archives/race/cb12-182.html.

"Courtroom History." Loving Day. 2012. http://www.lovingday.org/courtroom-history

"Down Syndrome Facts." National Down Syndrome Society. 2012. http://www.ndss.org/Down-Syndrome/Down-Syndrome-Facts/

"Unforgettable Change: 1960s: Civil Rights Marches Against Hiring Practices." Oakland Museum of California. http://www.museumca.org/picturethis/timeline/unforgettable-change-1960s/civil-rights/info

Orfield, Gary, and Jongyeon Ee. *Segregating California's Future: Inequality and Its Alternative 60 Years After Brown vs. Board of Education.* The Civil Rights Project: 2014. http://civilrightsproject.ucla.edu/research/k-12-education/integration-and-diversity/segregating-california2019s-future-inequality-and-its-alternative-60-years-after-brown-v.-board-of-education/orfield-ee-segregating-california-future-brown-at.pdf

Orfield, Gary, Erica Frankenberg, Jongyeon Ee, and John Kuscera. *Brown at 60: Great Progress, a Long Retreat and an Uncertain Future.* The Civil Rights Project: 2014. http://civilrightsproject.ucla.edu/research/k-12-education/integration-and-diversity/brown-at-60-great-progress-a-long-retreat-and-an-uncertain-future/Brown-at-60-051814.pdf

Orfield, Gary, John Kuscera, and Genevieve Siegel Hawley. *E Pluribus...Separation: Deepening Double Segregation for More Students: Executive Summary.* UCLA Civil Rights Project: 2012. http://civilrightsproject.ucla.edu/research/k-12-education/integration-and-diversity/mlk-national/e-pluribus...separation-deepening-double-segregation-for-more-students/

Rubin, Lillian. B. *Busing and Backlash: White Against White in an Urban School District.* Berkeley, CA: University of California Press. 1972.

Listed as Other

Leonard Haller

I love Chinese food. It's incredibly savory and arose from a place overflowing with rich culture. Yet there's always one haunting phenomenon that casts a shadow over me in every Chinese restaurant: the waiter always brings me a fork. I have a Caucasian face, so as soon as I walk through the doors the waiting staff always seem to assume that I have no idea how to use chopsticks. However courteous and "understanding" the waiter is trying to be, this simple action is presumptuous. My Malaysian mother spent many frustrating years teaching me the art of chopsticks in order to eat Asian cuisine properly. Her dedication to our culture made me proud of my Asian heritage, but my appearance is not at all associated with Asia and the ability to use chopsticks. Instead, I'm handed the devil's pitchfork that serves as an annoying reminder of just how un-Asian I appear.

As of fall 2013, I'm an undergraduate student at UCLA studying to become a physician. I was born in Germany to a German father and Chinese-Malaysian mother, but I have an overall Caucasian countenance. During my first few days of college, people were shocked to hear that I was Asian. I appear strictly white, and therefore I understood my initial categorization. At the same time, it's saddening to think that whenever I introduce myself to a peer, I'm immediately judged to be only white. I grew up surrounded by Chinese culture: I celebrated Chinese New Year and many other Chinese festivals, visited my maternal family in Malaysia countless times, and even played sports like Sepak Takraw, a Southeast Asian foot-volleyball game. This enormous portion of my background and upbringing is completely invisible to other people, and that can't ever be changed. And unfortunately, the way people initially see me won't either. This has always been the nature of contemporary society, and this trend has followed me even into UCLA.

The UCLA campus is amazingly diverse, listed as the eleventh most diverse school in the nation by *U.S. News & World Report* with a diversity index of 0.71 (with a maximum of 1.0) (US News, 2016). This index is based on the ratios of 34.8 percent Asian/Pacific Islander, 27.8 percent white, 18.0 percent Hispanic, 11.8 percent international, and 3.8 percent Black communities (UCLA Quick Facts, 2014). These ratios corroborate UCLA's claim of being one of the nation's most diverse campuses. It's a great example of an integrative community where all races have gathered to prepare for their futures. Students from many different ethnic backgrounds feel fully qualified and capable of competing at the rigorous academic level, and they're all fueled by the common goal of success and the hope for a fruitful career. However, although UCLA proves to be a highly integrative campus, there are still unintentional social barriers.

The idea of multiethnicity is relatively new. The population of mixed peoples is still relatively small, but it's growing exponentially, especially in such a cosmopolitan place like California. The recent 2010 census states that California now has 1.8 million people listed under two or more races, which is about 4.9 percent of the current population (US Census Bureau, 2010). Despite the prominence of multiethnicity, there is no social category that includes this increasing group of people. This is because racial categories stem from states or geographical regions where people unanimously identify and appear as a single ethnicity, but this nation doesn't exist for people of mixed races. Furthermore, multiethnicity is such an encompassing term; there is no precise category that these people fit into. Looking again at the percentages of races at UCLA, what would a multiethnic person check as they enter into UCLA? The program doesn't allow one to select multiple options, forcing many applicants to list themselves as the "other" option-- a twisted and ironic coincidence. This broad term could mean almost anything, and it causes people of mixed race to lose pride and self-identify. When people ask me where I'm from, I don't want to say "other."

Because of the novelty of multiethnicity, it hasn't appeared in many history books yet. When students learn about the past, they study Chinese empires and British imperialism. These are all distinct nationalities that have created well-established states, and therefore people can easily create social categories based on which of these countries someone appears to be from. Mixed race people are far too diverse to create their own establishment, and therefore it's not recognized as a social identity. So, in effect, my peers at UCLA don't look at me and initially wonder what sort of mix I could be. They see my white skin and instantly think European, or white. Mixed race is too new of an idea, and its population is still small.

Despite our few numbers, stereotypes have still risen that are associated with being mixed. I interviewed several students about their initial thoughts when I asked them about mixed races. One response I received was, "They're really hot" (In discussion with the author, May 26, 2014). This comment may seem like a compliment to some people, but to others it can be perceived in a multitude of different ways. It's a dangerous stereotype with the potential to offend many subgroups of people. The student being interviewed did not have malevolent intentions; it was just an honest opinion. The student also commented that he has no association with racism and has not had a prior confrontation based on his comments towards mixed groups. This is a recurring theme at UCLA. Students here are very accepting of others, and have no problem becoming friends and associating themselves with people of other races. However, there are still racist stereotypes and passive-aggressive comments that arise. For example, I have a group of peers who have a tendency to call me a Nazi because of my German heritage. There is no spite behind these comments; it's just meant as playful mockery. However innocent the comment may seem, this is still a form of unintentional discrimination, otherwise known as a microaggression. I don't associate with the Nazi party in any way, and just because I appear as white and have German roots it somehow leads to an extreme linkage with the Nazi party. Furthermore, my Chinese roots are completely overshadowed because of my appearance. Again, this is a contemporary example demonstrating that the way history students are taught impacts their social views. The effects of the Nazi Party are still a very prevalent topic today and they resonate in the present, leading to these harmful stereotypes of German people.

Additionally, being mixed race at UCLA carries the unfortunate consequence of unspoken social barriers. Upon entering the school, I wanted to join a club for Asian American students. I had heard it was a close-knit group of people that would constantly host social and engaging events. It appeared as a fantastic social opportunity for networking and creating relationships based upon cultural similarity. Upon going to the first meeting, many eyes turned towards me, as I was the only person there who appeared to be white. I instantly felt alienated and uncomfortable. This was a well-established club with a large amount of members, but I still didn't feel welcome there. I don't doubt that every member there was amicable, but I was incredibly intimidated that I couldn't find anyone who appeared to be anything but full Asian. These clubs have developed into groups that identify as one unified body of people who are all Asian. As a result, people who see themselves as multiple ethnicities are unintentionally ostracized. It's not the fault of the club; it's just that these clubs identify themselves under one specific social category, which poses a barrier to those who identify themselves as more. It's disheartening to know that if I just appeared Chinese, I would feel so much more comfortable joining the club without every pair of eyes turned towards me.

Overall, UCLA does have a relatively integrated community, but there are still unintentional social barriers that inhibit and can damage mixed race students. It's due to the small size of the multiethnic population, as well as the educational and cultural upbringing of this generation of students. It's a problem that still has no solution, and may only be fixed with time. The mixed community is growing substantially each year, and as time moves the idea of multiethnicity will become fully integrated into society. Hopefully, this group of people will be recognized and slowly these social boundaries will disappear. Personally, I consider myself lucky to be mixed race. I grew up surrounded by two incredibly rich cultures, and I'm very fortunate to have had this cultural immersion. In the real world however, it's been nothing but crippling. I'm both German and Chinese, and that's how I see myself. But to the rest of the world, I'm just listed as "other."

Bibliography

"Campus Ethnic Diversity: National Universities, 2015-2016 School Year."

U.S. News & World Report: 2016. https://www.usnews.com/best-colleges/rankings/national-universities/campus-ethnic-diversity

"Profile of General Population and Housing Characteristics." United States Census Bureau: 2010. https://factfinder.census.gov/faces/tableservices/jsf/pages/productview.xhtml?src=bkmk

"UCLA Undergraduate Admission: Quick Facts About UCLA." UCLA: 2014. http://www.admission.ucla.edu/campusprofile.htm

"Congratulations, You Look Like Me": Using my Multiracial Appearance to Uncover Views on Race, Status, and Beauty

Aislinn Dunne

Countless women have been stared at on the train. When this happens, it usually involves a pair of male eyes and a feeling of discomfort, but on a train from Beijing to Xi'an, a Chinese woman sat directly across from my brother and me, faced the two of us, and unabashedly looked from Caleb's face to mine. Eventually she turned to my mother and asked in Chinese, "Are they your children?" Upon confirmation that we were in fact related to my Chinese mother, the woman on the train declared that my brother looked more like my white father, and that I looked full Chinese. I acknowledged this observation with a neutral expression, not terribly surprised to hear that I looked like my own mother, and turned back to look out the window at the passing Chinese country side. When I eventually turned to glance back inside the train car, I found the two Chinese women staring expectantly at me. After an awkward pause, my mother gave the short, nervous laugh of a parent whose child had just said something slightly rude to a stranger and asked, "Aren't you going to say thank you?"

I have described my mixed heritage to many people, sometimes in response to being asked, "What are you?", and sometimes unsolicited by the listener. When people discover where my color comes from (China and the British Isles), the general reaction is a simple "Ah!" or "Oh, I see it now," like someone learning the answer to a riddle that has puzzled them for some time. But occasionally, observers will qualify their reactions to my race and appearance by prescribing positivity or negativity to how much I look like one race or another. Like the woman on the Chinese train, many people consider the appearance of one ethnic group to be more desirable than others, and thereby use a person's likeness to said ethnic group as a compliment rather than a simple observation. I have found that these associations of positivity or negativity to racial appearance reveal the views that people hold on race and beauty. By using physical traits indicative of specific ethnic groups as compliments or insults, people unknowingly use my looks and ethnic background to reveal various societal ideas about how race and color fit into what is considered desirable, high status, and beautiful.

In a politically correct utopia, being described as any given race would not be considered to be a compliment or insult, but rather an objective observation of which ethnicity a viewer sees when he or she looks at you. However, many do consider certain ethnic features to be better or more beautiful than others, and this attitude is often reflected in the way they talk about physical appearance. Because of our racially ambiguous appearances, multiracial people have a unique opportunity to see these attitudes more frequently than others. Friends and strangers alike discuss and analyze how our actual races match up with our physical appearance, and offer up their opinions on the degree to which they recognize our various ethnicities. In these conversations, which are supposedly centered on the mixed person, those making the commentary are providing insights into their own beliefs and the beliefs held by the cultural groups to which they belong. They unintentionally turn a discussion that they think is about a mixed person into an unveiling of their own views.

One view on race that has been revealed to me by such discussions is that of exclusivity. There are those who hold their own race in high regard, and have grown up to believe that being a member of that ethnic group is an attractive thing in and of itself. The woman on the Chinese train represents an attitude of Asian exclusivity in which being included in the world's largest national population is considered a highly selective compliment. A little on the narcissistic side, the general sentiment of, "You look like me; you're welcome" is one that shows that the speaker feels that he or she is giving a compliment when describing someone as part of his/

her own ethnic group. This is particularly meaningful to someone of mixed descent, for (as I have found in my interactions with full Asians) people with this attitude do not immediately accept mixed individuals as members of their community. To these people, membership into their ethnic community is to be earned, and anyone deemed to look like that ethnic group, especially someone who is not 100 percent the desired race, is deserving of high praise. It doesn't necessarily mean that the individuals making the judgment actually think that people of their own races are the most outwardly beautiful people in the world, but rather that inclusion in the community is a privilege, and that they are validating the mixed person by judging his/her physical features to reflect that ethnic group. This may explain why both my mother and the woman on the train sat patiently in their seats waiting for me to give thanks for the acknowledgement of my own heritage. While my mother may not consider her contribution to my phenotype to be any better than that of my father, she understood the implications of the other Chinese woman's "compliment" and instructed me to take it as such. Both the Chinese woman's remarks and my mother's understanding of their implications exemplify the tendency for some people to see their own race as more desirable than others.

While the woman on the train deemed my face worthy of entrance to the You-Look-Like-1.3-Billion-Other-People-In-This-Country Club, not all multiracial people gain such acceptance. This attitude of selectivity can alienate mixed people, marginalizing those who do not look "fully" like a certain ethnic group. Like many Hapas, I am frequently told by other Asians that I am not a "real Asian," a statement that is meant to reject biracials from the Asian community and shows an "all-or-nothing" approach to race that ultimately outcasts mixed people.

When I started high school, I moved to a new school district where I knew almost none of the other students. Meeting new people of course means explaining why some girl with an Irish surname is eating leftover stir-fry for lunch, or why a white man is picking up my tan, chopstick-using self from school. This led to a fresh batch of commentary about how my looks aligned with my heritage, and new opportunities for others to show their true opinions on race. One day, several of my friends were examining which of my physical features were more Asian and which were more European, a discussion that was interrupted by an Asian classmate stating flatly, "You look like a white girl." She claimed that she never would have guessed that I was anything but white unless I had informed her of my Chinese heritage. I have noticed that many people who share only one ethnicity with a biracial person tend to see the other ethnicity more clearly, as it is less familiar and stands out more to him/her. However, the hard stare and blunt tone of mild annoyance with which my classmate delivered her statement suggested that her views on my races were colored by her own ideas of what it meant to be white or Asian. Some Asians, including members of my family, openly laugh when I claim ties to Asia, finding it hysterical that I would identify even slightly (let alone 50 percent) with "their" people. These people exemplify an "all-or-nothing" approach to race, in which fractions are meaningless and half-white individuals either "make the cut" as an ethnic person or do not. Rather than seeing parts of different communities represented within a mixed person, they make a judgment about whether you are in or out of the group, an admissions process, which rivals that of any Ivy League university. The girl who claimed to see no Asian qualities in me was not really saying that my skin (darker than hers) looked like that of my English ancestors, or that my eyes (the same shape and color as my mother's) are bright blue. What she was really admitting was that she didn't see me as 100 percent Asian, and therefore saw zero Asian characteristics in me. Admitting that some parts of my appearance looked Asian and some parts looked European would require her to also admit that both qualities could exist in one person, a concept that does not fit in to the "all-or-nothing" approach to race.

Many people in our society have this need to place individuals into one and only one neat category. This is demonstrated at a larger societal scale with questionnaires that instruct mixed people to "check one box only" when defining their racial identities, or by people who ask multiracials, "But are you *more* [mom's race] or [dad's race]?" Humans, the species that brought you taxonomic classification and standardized tests, have a tendency to understand the world by categorizing and defining objects as fully one thing or another. This has served us well in figuring out similarities and differences between the materials that surround us, but when multiracial people enter the picture, the standard ethnic classifications that we have grown to understand are recombined, and some fail to grasp this racial remix. The monochromatic label that my classmate gave me in her flat and unamused tone shows that she belongs to this group of people who can only see one color at a time, and that she was quick to reject me from her own racial category.

While acceptance or rejection from a racial group based on appearance can show a sense of pride or elitism, it can also reveal feelings of inferiority, or the devaluing of one's own ethnicity. I and other half-Asians that I know have received comments from some full Asians such as "You're looking very handsome today—very pale" or "Sorry, but you look full Asian" or "No offence, but you've gotten really tan!" By congratulating us on our white features and apologizing for our darker ones, some Asians use Hapas to reveal either insecurity about their own race or to reflect cultural beauty standards. Qualifying otherwise neutral descriptions about our appearance with words like "sorry" or "no offence" suggests that the speaker believes these traits to be displeasing, and is therefore apologetic when he/she feels the need to offer up such observations. I do not find it offensive to hear that I have skin that is closer in color to my mother than to my father, but the remorseful way in which some full Asians describe my Asian features shows that they view European traits to be more beautiful or desirable than their own. In a society where the media sets beauty standards mostly with attractive white models and celebrities, I am not terribly surprised that a person of color would view European features as more attractive than those of an underrepresented ethnicity. As a foil to the Chinese woman on the train who praised the traits that I shared with her, it is a bit discouraging to hear others apologize to me for looking like them.

Assigning negativity to Asian features and positivity to paleness is indicative of a group of people that finds European features to be more desirable traits than those of their own ethnicity. This beauty standard is present in many cultures, manifesting itself in skin-whitening creams in Kenya and eyelid-doubling surgeries in East Asia. Historically, pale skin has been associated with higher socio-economic status as it indicated higher-paying indoor professions rather than manual outdoor labor. And with the rise of European imperialism in the early eighteenth century, white Europeans became the politically and economically powerful class in colonies full of non-white natives. The link between dark skin and manual or agricultural labor, combined with a history of European colonialism, has created an association of pale skin or European features with wealth and power that still carries on and manifests itself in today's beauty standards.

As the weather turns warm in the spring and solar radiation starts ramping up its summertime attack, I often hear my Korean or Indian friends lamenting about how tan they are getting. We live in California, a state where Hollywood actors and actresses risk skin cancer to beef up their melanin count in tanning salons, and even though we are far from British-occupied Asia of the 1800s or the rural farmlands of China, the idea that tans are bad still persists. These complaints show yet another idea about beauty: that whiteness in non-white people is desirable. My friends of color who grieve over the tans that they develop whilst walking to class in the omnipresent Los Angeles sunshine, or who say, "No offense, but you got really dark!" after I come back from a trip to the beach, are all expressing a preference for pale skin in people who are naturally darker.

In Southern California, this stands in stark contrast to the bikini-clad blondes who carve out time in their day to lay themselves out in the sun trying to darken their skin tone. Girls with pale skin complexions will often compliment me on my tan, telling me how lucky I am to have the dark, sundrenched look that they wish they could achieve. Their envy reflects the inverse of those who tell me things like, "No offense, but you're really dark!" The white girls who look wistfully at my skin tone (apparently white mixed with yellow turns brown in the sun) are subscribers to the idea that a tan looks healthy and implies outdoor activity. In a middle to upper class American context, tans no longer symbolize physical labor, but rather taking beach vacations and playing tennis on outdoor courts. These two views on skin tone, each of which is steeped in its own historical and social background, are exposed by the way in which people comment on my appearance.

There is one thing that people with these opposing views on tans have in common. It is the same thing that our woman on the Chinese train has in common with my friend who felt pity for me because of my prevalent Asian features. It is the same thing that ties the strangers who compliment me on looking more like my mother's side of the family with my classmate who refused to believe that one of my parents is not white. The thing that all of these people, and every person in the world for that matter, have in common is that when they meet me, they are presented with the same person. I do not change my hair for those who think that they hold the power to validate or delegitimize my ethnicities. I wear the same clothes in front of people who recognize both sides of my heritage as I do in front of people who wish to assign me only one racial label. My skin looks the same to those who see dark skin tones as a badge of the working class as it does to those who risk skin cancer to look like they live at the beach. The variation in commentary about how my race relates to my appearance is not a true unbiased measure of the link between my genotype and phenotype. Instead, it is an exposé of how people associate race and skin color with status and beauty. The different qualities that others see in me are all there, but are selected for or ignored depending on the personal views and biases that the others themselves hold. As a mixed person, I have the privilege of tasting from the giant ethnic sampler plate of culture that is my own background, but I also get the unique opportunity to sample an even larger variety of cultural and societal ideas about ethnicity by conversing about my own heritage with others. When the strangers and friends in my life discuss my race, they are of course under the impression that the conversation is about me, and that my looks, background, and identity are the only things being analyzed. But through their comments, qualifying remarks, complimentary or insulting tones, and assignments of positivity or negativity to my race and appearance, the speakers reveal so much more about themselves than they discover about me. The more they dissect and make remarks about me, the more I learn about their own views on the world. My multiracial face opens up a window into the viewpoints of many groups of people and allows me to gain a better understanding of their true feelings on color and beauty. This is a window that people will continue to unknowingly open throughout my life, and I can only guess what new perspectives I will gain on my next train ride.

Finding Lenses for My Myopic Green-Tinted Almond Eyes: My First Year as a Teaching Assistant

Emily H.A. Yen

Part One: Finding Lenses for My Myopic Green-Tinted Almond Eyes

I was fourteen the first time I tried putting contact lenses in. I wanted to start high school with them and not have fogged up glasses whenever I ate soup or sweated during a run.

My mother prepaid for a year's worth of contact lenses, but I had to get them in my eyes before I got my supply.

Most people can get them in a single teaching lesson within twenty to thirty minutes. I couldn't. I tried until my eyes turned red and was told to come back next week.

When I returned, I told the optometry assistant that I thought they were too big for my eyes and she told me that plenty of Asian people were able to get them in their eyes.

My instructor's patience turned into impatience at some point each session. Each week the tipping point became sooner. She we would always attribute my failure to lack of hand-eye coordination, length of my fingernails, and my general lack of effort. I wanted them badly and would practice my eye exercises religiously. I even tried to surreptitiously watch my younger brother take his contacts in and out to see if I was missing anything.

I went back at least a dozen times. Finally, the instructor became so disgusted that she made me sit in the corner of the lobby and spent most of the hour taunting me. Telling me that if I really wanted contact lenses I would be able to put them in.

I didn't go back for six years.

When I graduated from college I earnestly returned to the same optometry store. I wanted to wear contact lenses to my first job. I just found out that they had just implemented a three-session policy limit.

The sessions didn't go much better than the first. After my third session ended red watery eyes and a defeated spirit. Their several year overdue refund was the only consolation.

Part Two: Take Two

When I came to UCLA as a graduate student in sociology I was still determined to get contact lenses. So I found an optometrist in Westwood who specialized in custom lenses for people who couldn't wear normal ones. Dr. Vogel was gentle and grandfatherly. He did a comprehensive exam of my eyes and used a special device to measure the topography of my eyes. I found that my teenage intuition was correct.

I had -7.5 eyes.

A severe stigmatism.

Exceptionally steep corneas.

With openings no wider than an infant's.

Dr. Vogel ordered some custom made ones. A week later, when they arrived, I was able to get them in my first lesson. I couldn't stop smiling. I gave the optometrist a hug and literally skipped out of the office. Then I took a bunch of selfies.

Even at twenty-four, I was proud of my contact lenses. It was hard to fully explain my utter rapture to my new classmates, since it didn't take most people a decade to learn how to wear contacts.

Part Three: Graduate Student Funding and Teaching Assistantships at UCLA

There's a tacit understanding to avoid talking about fellowships, discussing specifics, at least until you know someone well. Eventually, students become curious about whose teaching the next year and the topic inevitably got brought up. People sheepishly mention the fellowship they had won and then the other person congratulates them. Sometimes it's genuine congratulation; other times it's jealousy wrapped-up in faux-congratulations.

When I got admitted to UCLA, I had received the Cota-Robles Fellowship, a prestigious fellowship that included three years of fellowship and two years of teacher assistantship (TA-ship) that started during my third year. There's an unspoken understanding to avoid talking about it, or discussing specifics, or at least until you know someone well enough. Eventually, students become curious. Eventually, though, students become curious, graduate students start to become curious especially as they realize this very thing: that some students have to TA second year while others don't. That starts discussions. It's a delicate topic since neither party wants to appear boastful or shortchanged.

A friend who I spent a good deal of time with finally broached the topic midway through my first year. Indirectly, of course. We were alone, walking back from class when he asked me if I was going to be TA'ing next year. I told him, no, that I would be on fellowship and then he asked me which one. So I told him . . . He then asked me if it was diversity related. I said "yes."

He immediately told me that it was kind of random how that worked out since I was half Asian and half white and came from an upper middle class background and thus didn't have anything in my background that would indicate disadvantage.

I was stunned.

Stunned because this was my friend. Stunned that he had espoused progressive values and at that moment appeared very closed minded.

Instantly, I felt a mixture of frustration and shame. I was frustrated that my friend was attributing my accolade to chance, completely diminishing the value of my academic accomplishments. My cheeks burned with shame as I said "like" too many times when searching for the words to succinctly explain why I was deserving of my fellowship. At that point, I knew him well enough to privately discuss funding packages but not well enough to reveal that I hadn't been a high achieving student for most of my life. I felt like an imposter.

The word "disability" was on the tip of my tongue but I felt too naked using it. There was no way to acknowledge my socioeconomic privilege and explain the individual and structural discrimination I endured on a daily basis for most of my K-12 education. To state that my parents' socioeconomic status certainly mitigated, but in no way cancelled, the effects of my learning disability. I wanted to say something pithy about the intersectionality of race and disability, that students of Asian descent are often under diagnosed for learning disabilities, but red-hot shame overtook me.

I eventually mumbled that there were other types of diversity and changed the topic. I couldn't stop thinking about it.

Even though I didn't owe him an explanation, I felt shame for keeping a piece of myself private and not using this as an opportunity to correct stereotypes and combat oppression. I simultaneously was and was not a high-achieving student of color from an affluent background.

Despite scoring a verbal aptitude in the ninety-ninth percentile, I couldn't read independently until after my ninth birthday or write a cogent essay until after my fifteenth. I had my hearing surgically corrected and went to speech therapy until high school. When I got retested on adult norms, my reading fluency and reading comprehension were separated by six standard deviations. The psychologist who was testing me told me that in the twenty years in his career, he hadn't seen a disparity so large and was genuinely baffled how I functioned academically at Smith, a prestigious liberal arts college where Sylvia Plath, Gloria Steinem, and Julia Child all hailed from. A couple years later, in between college and grad school, I took a job at a publishing house in New York. I felt proud coming into the office every day, feeling lucky to work in an industry that I was told countless times that I wouldn't be good at.

Part Four: Socioeconomic Class and My Early Years

Socioeconomic class is something hard to categorize, especially when level of education and income don't match up. We lived in a Victorian fixer-upper in an affluent suburb of Boston. Both of my parents graduated from college. My father is a physician who had taught at Harvard during my early childhood. I never thought about money much, even though he was supporting six people on a junior faculty salary. He moonlighted on the weekends in the emergency room so he could put money in four children's

529 Plans. My mom took care of me, and my three brothers, and ferried us to gymnastics, archery, and art classes at the Museum of Fine Arts in Boston.

After my parents split up when I was eight, money was extremely tight for a number of years. My mother couldn't find work as a nurse, and ended up working at a grocery store for several months. I remember the silent humiliation of browsing in an expensive furniture store, knowing we couldn't afford anything, and knowing that the store clerk knew that too.

I think I felt the duality most acutely in middle school. My parents resided in two different states, two and a half hours apart, and shuttled us back and forth every weekend.

We ended up moving to Charlottesville, Virginia. Actually, I lived in an unincorporated part of the county several miles outside of the city line. In the late 1990s the county was still pretty rural and was a very much a Black-white area. I had to constantly explain that I was half Chinese and half Polish, but was fully American. Both of my parents were born in the United States. Even though I didn't strongly resemble my Caucasian mother, I was flummoxed why I was asked if I was adopted so many times, especially by teachers. If I were hypothetically adopted, why would I retain the Chinese surname?

I remember in seventh grade being humiliated on a five day field trip to a marine biology center, when a classmate asked me how I could afford to go on this trip since I wore clothes from Sears. With flushed cheeks and deep shame, I couldn't find the words to explain: that my parents valued education and wanted me to learn more about water salinity and tide pools, that they had always deemphasized material things and spent the bulk of their discretionary income on educational activities, that I preferred to go clothes shopping with my mother, who had far less discretionary income. Instead, I just told her that I wasn't poor; my dad was a doctor. She eyed me skeptically, and asked again why I got my clothes from Sears.

My home life settled some when I got to high school. My mom moved back to a DC suburb, within a five mile radius of my dad. It was a very ethnically diverse area, where many of my friends' parents worked at the National Institute of Health (NIH). I joined the cross-country team and started to make friends. I still remember the glee I felt during the first week of school when a girl invited me to go to the mall with her. She was half Chinese and half Caucasian.

I felt like I belonged for the first time in a long time.

But I felt like I was waging war with one teacher or another almost every single day in high school. There were other high achieving students with learning disabilities in my school, but mine was often considered difficult to accommodate since it was classified as "non-standard." I had many teachers who assumed that I didn't really have a learning disability and told me that they thought my parents hired a psychologist to help me gain an academic advantage. Others thought it was too much work to accommodate me and felt like I didn't belong in Advanced Placement classes.

My academic performance suffered since I was asked to perform tasks no other student was asked to. Almost every day I had to try and schedule time to finish a quiz, test, or in-class assignment without being late to my next class. I tried to find a mutually convenient time to finish an assignment, often weeks after I started it. It was difficult to retain large amounts of information for these tests when I had several quizzes and tests to study for in between the start and finish time. I regularly deprived myself of sleep in order to take six AP classes my senior year.

Smith took a chance on me and accepted me early decision. I jumped up and down wildly when I received that fat envelope in the mail.

Going to Smith helped me become the person I wanted to become. It was really my professors who helped me get there, tenderly guiding me to possibilities that I could not see. I'm especially indebted to my undergraduate advisor, Nancy Whittier, who line-edited my first conference paper five times over winter break. She met with me every single week for two years, and helped me get into a top PhD Program.

Part Five: My First Year as a Teaching Assistant at UCLA

Reading remains a challenge for me as a graduate student. Like most of my fellow classmates, I spend most of my time reading, but I often have to re-read an article three times in order to fully absorb it. Nonetheless, I am no longer embarrassed by my academic struggles that I've endured and presently face.

During my third year of graduate school at UCLA, I became a teaching assistant in the sociology department. It was overwhelming to try and learn the names of seventy-five students at the beginning of the quarter while studying for my field exams. However, it was also exhilarating to be able to guide students.

For the first time I was in a position to hold other peoples' hands and extend them the patience and kindness that was afforded to me—by my mother, my father, my undergraduate advisor, my optometrist, and many others. I try to honor them by doing my best, my absolute best, to be generous with my time and learn my students' strengths, help them overcome their weaknesses, and celebrate their successes. For their first essay, I line- edited all seventy-five essays. It was a colossal expenditure of time but I knew it would help them, or at least some of them, find their lenses.

About the Editors

Robert Chao Romero is Associate Professor of Chicana/o Studies and Asian-American studies at UCLA. His book, The *Chinese in Mexico 1882-1940* (2010), tells the forgotten history of the Chinese community in Mexico and received the Latina/o Studies Section Book Award from the Latin American Studies Association.

James Ong is a writer based in San Jose, California. He is a twin of mixed Chinese and Caucasian heritage and earned a master's degree in Asian American Studies from UCLA.

Dr. Chelsea Guillermo-Wann is an educator dedicated to equity and social justice for all students, with expertise in intergroup relations, campus climate for diversity, and multiraciality. She earned her Ph.D. in Higher Education and Organizational Change from UCLA.

Jenifer Logia graduated from UCLA with a degree in International Development Studies and Asian American Studies, and holds a Master's in Public Policy from Mills College. In 2013, she co-founded the annual Mixed Heritage Conference at UCLA, and in 2015 founded the nation's first-ever Mixed Alumni Association.

www.ingramcontent.com/pod-product-compliance
Lightning Source LLC
Chambersburg PA
CBHW020858090426
42736CB00008B/416